E-Etiquette

Skyhorse Publishing books may be purchased in bulk at special discounts for sales promotion, corporate gifts, fund-raising, or educational purposes. Special editions can also be created to specifications. For details, contact the Special Sales Department, Skyhorse Publishing, 307 West 36th Street, Floor 11, New York, NY 10018 or info@skyhorsepublishing.com.

www.skyhorsepublishing.com

10 9 8 7 6 5 4 3 2 1

Library of Congress Cataloging-in-Publication Data is available on file.

Print ISBN: 978-1-62914-574-7

Printed in China

NATIONAL LEAGUE OF COTILLIONS™

~

E-ETIQUETTE

THE DEFINITIVE GUIDE TO PROPER MANNERS IN TODAY'S DIGITAL WORLD

CHARLES AND ANNE WINTERS, ELIZABETH ANNE RUSSELL, AND CHARLES WINTERS II

Skyhorse Publishing

CONTENTS

INTRODUCTION

During the past few years, we have become engulfed in a tidal wave of technology. It has greatly accelerated the speed of communication, given instant access to data, and made life more convenient. At the same time, society has been drowning in a sea of information overload and time pressure that often results in rudeness and incivility.

Every year the National League of Cotillions teaches etiquette, social skills, and character education to thousands of students of all ages—from pre-kindergarten to adults. In the process, we have learned that courtesy must extend far beyond face-to-face encounters. For example, what you say in a text message or a voice mail reflects your personality as much as a handshake. As you will discover, manners are equally as important as machines.

The topics of this book are presented in a question-answer format:

- ❖ When is using a cell phone inappropriate?
- ❖ What should I do if it is absolutely necessary to take incoming calls in a public place?
- ❖ What limits should be placed on the use of a home computer by family members?
- ❖ Are there specific courtesies when using video and digital cameras?
- ❖ How can I help keep my cell phone from disturbing my schedule?
- ❖ What courtesies apply to social networking?

❖ What guidelines should be observed when replying to an e-mail message?

❖ What is the correct way to answer a phone call at home?

❖ What are the "Seven W's" of taking phone messages?

❖ What electronic courtesies are expected on airplanes and in restaurants?

❖ What rules should be established for music in the home?

❖ What is considered good etiquette for leaving messages on someone's business voice mail?

❖ Is there a gracious way to shorten a call? And how should it be concluded?

❖ What are the basic rules to follow when faxing?

❖ Should children have their own telephones?

You will find answers to these questions, and more.

The final chapter presents a parent-child guide to electronic etiquette—including the use of home computers, phones, music, DVDs, digital games, and more. We emphasize the importance of setting boundaries for children at an early age. The principles you establish are building blocks that will shape their character and attitude for a lifetime.

It is our sincere desire that this book will help you, your family, and your associates keep the focus on good manners and courtesy in this electronic age.

—*Charles, Anne, Elizabeth Anne,* and *Charles Winters II.*

*W*HAT IS
CONSIDERED
GOOD ETIQUETTE
FOR LEAVING
MESSAGES ON
SOMEONE'S
BUSINESS VOICE
MAIL?

ONE

CELL PHONE COURTESIES

Professional golfer John Cook was about to taste victory. He was tied for the lead on the seventeenth hole of the Sony Open at the Waialae Country Club in Honolulu, Hawaii.

Then, on his backswing at the par-three hole, a cell phone began to ring near the tee box. The sound distracted Cook, and the shot ended up in a bunker near the green. Clearly upset, the 10-time winner on the PGA tour grumbled, "Ahhhhhh! Whose cell phone?"

Cook bogeyed the hole and lost the tournament to Jerry Kelly by one stroke. Instead of a $720,000 payday, his second-place finish reduced his winnings to $432,000. That was an expensive cell phone call!

Even more disturbing, as one witness recounted, "The thoughtless spectator answered the phone and started talking!"

For better or for worse, the rapid proliferation of wireless phones has revolutionized the way people communicate with each other. They not only keep individuals in constant contact, but also are invaluable in emergencies.

Over half of the people in the United States use cell phones daily. Parents keep in touch with their children and executives talk with their fast-paced associates.

Unfortunately, many users of mobile phones have developed habits that have been described as rude, ill-mannered, and discourteous. Some medical doctors are reporting cases of "cell phone rage" that have resulted in black eyes and broken bones.

Today, an increasing number of restaurants have established "cell-free" zones. In Europe, many trains have phone-free sections.

The National League of Cotillions has established the following ways to master productivity and politeness when using your cell phone.

The National League of Cotillions has established the following ways to master productivity and politeness when using your cell phone.

Stay Safe

*B*e alert and use your wireless phone to help others in emergencies. According to the Cellular Telecommunications Industry Association (CTIA), cell phones are used approximately 400,000 times every day in the U.S. to dial 911 and other emergency numbers. They help to save lives and to report other dangerous situations.

How can one have a safer cell phone experience while driving?

A Toronto study reported in the New England Journal of Medicine found that the risk of an automobile accident quadruples when talking on a cell phone. The distraction caused by the device has been named by Harvard University's Center for Risk Analysis as the reason for a half million crashes and more than 3,300 highway deaths each year. As a result, most states have some type of law and/or restriction regarding mobile phone use while operating a motor vehicle. New York was the first state to totally ban cell phone use by drivers. Many other states have followed in their footsteps. To find the policy in your state, visit: www.ghsa.org/html/stateinfo/laws/cellphone_laws.html.

You show consideration for others when you take responsibility for the manner in which you use a wireless phone while driving.

You will stay much safer and show respect by following these important rules:

- ❖ Inform the person you are speaking with that you are driving (in case you are disconnected).
- ❖ If you must talk while driving, use voice-activated dialing, an earpiece, and a clip-on or sun visor microphone. Better yet, have a hands-free phone installed in your car by a professional.
- ❖ Don't try to put your earpiece on while driving.
- ❖ Make it a habit to find a safe place to stop before dialing (unless you have voice-activated dialing).
- ❖ Keep your hands on the wheel and your eyes on the road.

MAKE IT A HABIT TO FIND A SAFE PLACE TO STOP BEFORE DIALING (UNLESS YOU HAVE VOICE-ACTIVATED DIALING).

❧

- ❖ Remember that changing lanes and tapping a cell phone keypad are not compatible.
- ❖ Know your phone well enough to activate it quickly.
- ❖ Use speed dialing (or one-touch redial) whenever possible.
- ❖ Never take notes or look up phone numbers while driving.
- ❖ Suspend calls in heavy traffic or during hazardous weather.
- ❖ Avoid stressful phone conversations while driving.
- ❖ Never use your phone in congested traffic areas.

Better yet, follow the advice of a bumper sticker distributed by a radio station: "Drive Now, Talk Later."

If you find it necessary to use your phone while driving, make it a habit to get in your car, buckle up, and prepare your voice-activated phone, earpiece, or hands-free device before starting your engine.

In addition to driving, are there additional safety issues involved with cell phones?

*N*ever attempt to use a cell phone while on an airplane since it can cause interference with sensitive radio transmission. The exception, of course, is if there is a situation that needs to be

*N*EVER TAKE NOTES OR LOOK UP PHONE NUMBERS WHILE DRIVING.

reported to officials. Also avoid using your phone in hospitals — especially near an emergency room or surgery area. It may affect patient monitoring devices and even heart pacemakers.

SHOW RESPECT

Is it impolite to use your cell phone in the company of associates or friends?

*W*hen you take a call in the presence of a special client or personal friend, you are communicating, "You are secondary—the caller is more important than you."

If you are expecting an important call, let the person know in advance, and excuse yourself before taking the call, which should be kept very brief. If the conversation requires longer than one minute, arrange for a more convenient time to complete the call. Also:

❖ Avoid calling someone on his or her cell phone without prior permission. Remember, that person is paying for incoming calls.

❖ Do not receive a call when someone has an appointment with you—or when you have guests. It's rude!

❖ Remember to charge your batteries. It is not polite for a conversation to be interrupted due to low power.

AVOID CALLING SOMEONE ON HIS OR HER CELL PHONE WITHOUT PRIOR PERMISSION. REMEMBER, THAT PERSON MAY BE PAYING FOR INCOMING CALLS.

❖ Never use a cell phone on a date. It shows disrespect to your companion. Turn off the phone unless you are expecting an emergency call.

❖ Don't ignore the waitperson in a restaurant or a retail clerk because you are using your cell phone. You are infringing on that individual's valuable time.

❖ If you are on a speaker phone, always inform the person you are talking with. It respects their privacy.

Parents, if your children are involved in sporting events, give them your full attention. This is not a time to conduct business or chat with friends. Give your children the respect they deserve.

And one more note of caution: Don't be the person who talks in a noisy room with his or her finger in one ear—then reaches out to shake hands with an associate! It is unhygienic.

NOTE: When you are in a public place, it is polite to answer your phone as soon as possible in order not to disturb those around you.

If you are on a speaker phone, always inform the person you are talking with. It respects their privacy.

HONOR PRIVACY

Why don't people understand that I would prefer not to overhear their cell phone talk?

People are often embarrassed when they hear one-sided conversations regarding health issues, family problems, or business deals.

Honor the privacy of others:

- ❖ Never call during mealtimes, early morning, or late at night.
- ❖ Do not make important business decisions from a cell phone in a public place.
- ❖ Golf courses and sporting events are places to get away from business. Turn off your phone.
- ❖ Always assume that someone may eavesdrop on your conversation.

In a public restroom, a gentleman dialed a cell phone number and, in a loud voice, asked, "Hi, how you doing?" The person in the next stall responded, "Just fine, thank you!"

SPEAK QUIETLY

Why do people tend to speak loudly while using a cell phone?

*M*any individuals fail to realize that a mobile phone is a high-tech instrument that will operate properly even if you speak in a lower than normal voice tone.

- ❖ Don't yell! Let the phone do the work.
- ❖ Turn your incoming audio volume to maximum. When you hear well, you will speak softer.
- ❖ Learn to use text messaging (discussed later in this chapter and in Chapter Three).

ALWAYS ASSUME THAT SOMEONE MAY EAVESDROP ON YOUR CONVERSATION.

Do not use your phone while eating a meal. Can you imagine what you sound like talking and chewing food at the same time—even with a hands-free microphone?

❖ Never call attention to yourself—by a loud ring, or a loud voice.

❖ If you are required to use your cell phone for a conference call, speak from a quiet location—never from a noisy atmosphere. You'll end up talking too loud.

❖ Do not use your phone while eating a meal. Can you imagine what you sound like talking and chewing food at the same time—even with a hands-free microphone?

❖ Never allow people close by to overhear your conversation.

❖ Never use a rap/pop song as a ringtone. You will be embarrassed if inappropriate lyrics blare from your purse or desk while your boss is near. Choose a classic, non-annoying ring. Select a volume appropriate for the setting. Do not leave the volume on max while you are indoors.

DON'T DISTURB

Recently, during a Broadway performance, an actor stopped the show when a cell phone rang and the patron began speaking. He asked the person to leave the theater and there was a standing ovation.

When is using a cell phone inappropriate?

In social and business situations, remember to turn off your phone. There is no rule that says you must constantly be "on call." Ask yourself, "Will my conversation disturb others?"

Never place or receive a call, or allow the phone to ring or beep, during a meal, meeting, religious service, wedding, or funeral. Be sure to turn your phone off, or switch to "vibrate," when in the theater, doctor's office, elevator, museum, library, or public restroom.

Some business firms are now asking clients to check their cell phones at the reception desk. And many school districts have rules that ban cell phones from the classroom. (They must be kept in lockers.) If parents need to reach their child at school, they should call the principal's office. Always be aware of your school's current cell phone policy and respect that decision.

Most courtrooms require that all cell phones be turned off.

❖ Explain in advance if you must answer your phone while in a social or business situation. Ask the caller to hold, then excuse yourself and exit the room before continuing the call.

❖ Use the vibrate feature whenever possible.

❖ If your phone is set on "ring," try to answer at the first sound.

❖ Set the ringtone at its lowest level.

EXPLAIN IN ADVANCE IF YOU MUST ANSWER YOUR PHONE WHILE IN A SOCIAL OR BUSINESS SITUATION.

Willie Brown, the former mayor of San Francisco, said, "The single most offensive thing you can do is come to a meeting with your cell phone on." A person witnessed a seminar participant actually crawl under a table to answer a call.

AIM FOR SILENCE

Take every precaution to make sure your phone is not aggravating others.

I'm sure you have heard a cell phone ring and have seen three or four people reach for their phones. The sound of the incoming call and the noise of the conversation can be annoying. This is why mobile units are being banned in so many places.

One organization set this rule: "The person whose cell phone goes off first buys lunch for the group!" People got the message.

It is difficult to find peace and quiet when wireless phone users are nearby.

- ❖ When people are present, use silent or vibrating options—or press "Power off."
- ❖ Caller ID allows you to see the caller's name and number before deciding whether you should excuse yourself and take the call.
- ❖ Become fully acquainted with the call forwarding and voice mail features of your phone.

CALLER ID ALLOWS YOU TO SEE THE CALLER'S NAME AND NUMBER BEFORE DECIDING WHETHER YOU SHOULD EXCUSE YOURSELF AND TAKE THE CALL.

- Screen every call and when in the presence of others only answer in an emergency.
- If you don't plan to take calls, turn the unit off. It is distracting to let the phone ring and ring and ring.
- Some professionals—such as medical doctors—must have their cell phones or beepers on at all times. They should use the silent options and seek privacy to take calls.

KEEP YOUR DISTANCE

How far should I move away from people before making a call?

Good manners require that you move to a location where others cannot hear your conversation. This is usually at least ten to fifteen feet away. Better yet, find a space that is totally private. If this is not possible, wait to make or take calls.

Also, when standing in an ATM line, back away from the person in front of you before using your phone.

GIVE AN EXPLANATION

What should I do if it is absolutely necessary to take incoming calls in a public place?

If you don't plan to take calls, turn the unit off. It is distracting to let the phone ring and ring and ring.

If you must keep your phone on, explain the reason to those around you. Say, "I am expecting an important call. I hope you will understand."

- ❖ If at a conference or a restaurant, sit near an exit.
- ❖ Place your phone on vibrator mode.
- ❖ Leave the room to take the call.

MANAGE YOUR TIME

How can I help keep my cell phone from disturbing my schedule?

Far too many people allow incoming calls to take precedent over almost every activity. It decreases their productivity and constantly disrupts their day. Here's how to avoid such problems.

- ❖ Whenever possible, use voice mail for incoming calls and return them at a convenient place and time.
- ❖ Keep your call time short.
- ❖ To decrease the number of incoming calls, do not give your cell phone number out freely.
- ❖ In your office, take calls at your desk, not while walking up and down the halls.
- ❖ Always let the other party know you are calling from a cell phone, in case the service is disrupted.

WHENEVER POSSIBLE, USE VOICE MAIL FOR INCOMING CALLS AND RETURN THEM AT A CONVENIENT PLACE AND TIME.

❖ Set aside specific, scheduled times to return calls on your voice mail.

Remember, you will be more productive by knowing the features of your phone. Practice the art of emergency use. Learn how to quickly access silent modes, voice mail, and more.

DON'T BE A SHOW-OFF

Why do some people use their cell phones to look and act important?

It's sad but true that some individuals actually ask people to call them—so they will look important. I'm sure you have seen those who have two or more electronic devices strapped to their belt. Hopefully, they have a good reason.

❖ Never use a cell phone to impress others.

❖ Don't try to dazzle people with your multitasking abilities.

❖ Don't wear your earpiece when not on the phone.

❖ Never place your cell phone on a restaurant table.

❖ Your phone is not a status symbol. It is merely a tool for communicating!

Also, unless you are a child, don't use novelty rings. No one likes to hear "Mary Had a Little Lamb" or "The Minute Waltz" blaring from your phone!

Don't try to dazzle people with your multitasking abilities.

Text Telephones

*E*very minute of every hour, millions of messages are being exchanged between wireless phones—not voice memos, but typed words that appear on tiny screens: "B HOME 7:30" or "CU TOMORROW."

The concept is not new. Text telephones were invented in the 1930s and were popular with journalists who could feed their stories directly to newspaper editors. Then, in the 1960s, Robert Weitbrecht, a deaf scientist, created a teletypewriter that allowed the hearing-impaired to communicate on existing telephone networks.

Today, instead of bulky units, we type on little handheld keyboards and retrieve messages on our beepers or wireless phones. Current script designers added the feature more as a novelty rather than a serious option. Now it has become an essential part of communication.

Text telephones (first in Europe and Asia, then the U.S.) began with personal use, but many in business and government find them extremely valuable. For example, airlines use them to relay flight information to gate agents.

Why has the short message service (SMS) text system become so popular?

❖ It's inexpensive, using less airtime than a voice call.

Today, instead of bulky units, we type on little handheld keyboards and retrieve messages on our beepers or wireless phones.

- ❖ It's convenient—forget about busy signals.
- ❖ It's discreet—you can send and receive messages at times when it is not appropriate to talk. For example: at sports events, on public transportation and at restaurants.

Cell phone text services deliver news, stock quotes, sports scores, and you can add literally thousands of applications—called "apps."

What abbreviations are acceptable when sending text messages?

*B*ecause the length of a text message may be limited (usually 160 units including spaces), people have become quite original in creating shortcuts.

In Chapter Three you will find symbols and abbreviations used in e-mail, but text messaging is creating a language all its own.

Since a single button on a cell phone numeric keypad has three or four letters, you may have to press more than once to enter the letter you need. Check the "T9 word" option. This allows you to type ABC characters. For example, if you want to say "Hi" you would hit 4 twice for the "H" and once more for the "I." Go to "options" on your cell phone or check the manual.

It only makes sense to press as few strokes as possible—that's why abbreviations seem so necessary.

CELL PHONE TEXT SERVICES DELIVER NEWS, STOCK QUOTES, SPORTS SCORES, AND YOU CAN ADD LITERALLY THOUSANDS OF APPLICATIONS— CALLED "APPS."

Here are just a few examples of how people shorten their words and sentences:

ATB	–	All the best.
B	–	Be.
BTW	–	By the way.
ENUF	–	Enough.
IN or N	–	Replaces "ing" word endings. For example: CALLN or DOIN.
IM	–	I am.
IMS	–	I am sorry.
INO	–	I know.
J4F	–	Just for fun.
MI	–	May I?
MIP	–	May I please?
NE1	–	Anyone.
NOM	–	No, Ma'am.
NS	–	No, Sir.
PC	–	Please call.
PME	–	Pardon me.
R	–	Are.
XLNT	–	Excellent.
YM	–	Yes, Ma'am.
YR	–	Your.
YS	–	Yes, Sir.

"N" REPLACES "ING" WORD ENDINGS. FOR EXAMPLE: CALLN OR DOIN.

In many cases, numbers replace words. For example, the number "2" replaces "to" or "too." You may enter 2DAY instead of "today." And 2G4U is used for "too good for you." The number "8" is used when a syllable sounds like "ate." L8ER means "later." GR8 means "great." W84ME is used for "wait for me."

When two people use mobile messaging to communicate with each other over long periods of time, their keystrokes become shorter and shorter—yet the communication remains clear.

A note of caution: When you purposely misspell you not only look ignorant, but it creates a bad habit. Examples are:

Kewl/Kool = Cool

Luve/Luv = Love

Skewl = School

Lyke = Like

Also avoid intentional capitalization errors. For example: WhEN pEopLE TyPe LiKe tHis, iT DriVEs ThEir rEAdEr InsANE!

In many cases, numbers replace words. For example, the number "2" replaces "to" or "too."

THE NATIONAL LEAGUE OF COTILLIONS OFFICIAL RULES OF CELL PHONE ETIQUETTE

❖ Stay safe. Before starting your engine, prepare your hand-free devices (voice activated dialing, earpieces, and clip-on microphones) to be used while driving.

Don't DISTURB. NEVER PLACE OR RECEIVE CALLS DURING A MEAL OR MEETING, OR IN A CHURCH, THEATER, COURT ROOM, OR PUBLIC EVENT.

Better yet, park your car before making or taking calls.

❖ Show respect. Those you are with should always take precedence over a call.

❖ Honor privacy. Never place calls during mealtimes, early morning, or late at night.

❖ Speak quietly. Keep your voice volume low.

❖ Don't disturb. Never place or receive calls during a meal or meeting, or in a church, theater, court room, or public event.

❖ Aim for silence. When others are present, use silent or vibrating options, or turn off the phone.

❖ Keep your distance. Move to a location where others cannot hear your conversation.

❖ Give an explanation. If you must keep your phone on, explain the reason to those around you.

❖ Manage your time. Whenever possible, use voice mail for incoming calls and return them at a convenient place and time.

❖ Don't be a show-off. Never use a cell phone to impress others.

TWO

PHONES AND DIGITAL MANNERS AT HOME

We have come a long way from March 10, 1876, when Alexander Graham Bell, the inventor of the telephone, made the first call to his assistant, Thomas Watson, who was in a nearby room. "Mr. Watson," he said, "come here. I want to see you."

That was the start of a revolution in communication that has linked our world together in unforeseen ways. However, the effective use of today's technology still depends on people who treat others with honor, dignity, and respect.

PHONE ETIQUETTE

The telephone is a vital communication tool. We use it every day to keep in touch with friends and relatives, make dinner or theater reservations, conduct banking and other business, and even register for college courses. And in times of emergency, the telephone is absolutely essential. But despite its many wonderful uses, the telephone can become a source of contention in your home.

Let's face it, we have all become irritated at times by:

❖ The sound of someone dialing while you are talking.

❖ A solicitor who interrupts the family dinner.

❖ A family member who stays on the phone too long.

❖ Trying to locate a misplaced cordless phone.

Don't despair! It is possible to have a phone-friendly home where communication hassles are kept to a minimum. The key is to have clear guidelines that are established by the head of the household and followed by every family member—including the children.

The four basic telephone rules, which we will discuss in this chapter, are:

❖ Set the hours and situations when you should and should not make or receive calls.

❖ Determine the maximum length of time for calls.

❖ Establish a specific style of answering and placing calls.

❖ Have an official message-taking system.

When reasonable rules and boundaries are understood and practiced, you'll find the phone becomes a friend—instead of a foe—in your home.

ESTABLISH A SPECIFIC STYLE OF ANSWERING AND PLACING CALLS.

PLUGGING IN

Just because the builder wired every room in your house with a phone jack doesn't mean you are required to install a dozen units. As you will see, there are locations where you should, and should not, have a phone.

Specifically, where should telephones be placed in the home?

*P*erhaps you have visited someone who has a phone in every room and when they all ring it sounds like a telethon or a switchboard center. The key here is to keep it simple. You don't need any more phones than are necessary.

Here is where they should be located:

- ❖ Telephones, either cordless or permanent, should be placed in the kitchen, master bedroom, home office, and guest bedroom.
- ❖ Install a phone close to (but not in) the family room, since calls might interfere with those engaged in conversation or other activities.
- ❖ Be sure the location is convenient and in a well-lighted place for taking messages.

What locations should be avoided when placing phones?

*D*o not have a phone in either the dining room or recreation room. Those areas are for other purposes.

*Y*OU DON'T NEED ANY MORE PHONES THAN ARE NECESSARY.

We do not recommend having telephones in the bedrooms of children in your home. We will discuss the reason in Chapter Seven.

PHONE TIMES

What time should calls be made—and what hours should be avoided?

*W*hen dialing someone's home, err on the safe side and don't call before 9 AM or after 9 PM. Also do not place calls during mealtimes. Honor the privacy of individuals unless they ask to be called during specific hours.

The exceptions to the recommended phone hours are (1) when prior arrangements have been made, and (2) when it is an emergency.

Always be aware of the time zone you are calling. Don't disregard the three-hour difference between Los Angeles and New York.

Should I answer the phone every time it rings?

A couple in Detroit was having a Sunday afternoon visit in the home of friends when the phone rang. "Aren't you going to answer that?" the visiting husband asked. "No," the host replied. "Having your company is much more important."

Always be aware of the time zone you are calling. Don't disregard the three-hour difference between Los Angeles and New York.

If the call is urgent, the person can leave a message on voice mail or the answering machine.

You are in control of the phone—the phone is not in control of you! Always ask yourself this question: What is more important, my current activity or this interruption? Who takes precedence, the person I am with or the person who is calling?

Also, don't answer the phone at mealtimes (and make sure the friends of your children know you do not take calls when the family is dining together). Let the call be received by voice mail or your answering machine.

Other times when you, or members of your family, should choose not to answer the phone include:

- ❖ Family time.
- ❖ When children are involved in homework or music practice.
- ❖ Quiet times when you are reading, reflecting, or even taking a nap.

YOU ARE IN CONTROL OF THE PHONE—THE PHONE IS NOT IN CONTROL OF YOU!

WATCH THE CLOCK

*B*oth incoming and outgoing calls should be kept to a fifteen-minute maximum—and much shorter when possible. Exceptions include when you are dealing with health issues, important personal matters, or having a conversation with an elderly person who may be lonely.

ANSWERING THE PHONE

*W*e believe the adage: "You never have a second chance to make a first impression." That is why the first words you say when picking up the receiver are so vital.

When the phone rings you may have no idea who has dialed—unless you have Caller ID—yet you need to answer with the same courtesy as if you knew the incoming call was from your best friend.

Receiving a call should be viewed as greeting someone in person. Focus on the individual and communicate joy and enthusiasm. It should always be a pleasure for the caller to hear your voice. Even though you may be in the middle of a major project, give the caller the impression that you are happy the phone rang. If you can't answer with a positive attitude, let the call go to voice mail or an answering machine.

After answering the phone properly, you might say, "Donna, how are you? I haven't heard from you in so long." Instead of just, "How's it going?"

You honor and respect others when you let them know how important they are—whether the call is for you, or for another person.

EVEN THOUGH YOU MAY BE IN THE MIDDLE OF A MAJOR PROJECT, GIVE THE CALLER THE IMPRESSION THAT YOU ARE HAPPY THE PHONE RANG.

What is the correct way to answer a phone call at home?

$\mathcal{T}$he ideal time to pick up the phone is between the third and fourth rings. Don't race to the phone, or you will sound as if you are out of breath. Also, answering on the first ring may rush—or even startle—the caller.

IMPROPER "Hello?"—and nothing more.

PROPER: "Hello, this is Mary Jones." Or, "Jones residence. This is Mary Jones speaking."

NOTE: When you are the guest in someone's home or you have been requested to answer the phone, ask how it should be answered. The recommended response is: "Taylor residence. Bill James speaking."

Teach even young children to answer the phone properly. Callers should always receive a polite greeting, even if received by your elementary school-aged child.

How should I respond if the call is for another person?

$\mathcal{R}$egardless of who the call is for, you should always answer in a calm, courteous manner. Don't give the impression you have imposed on their time and interrupted something important.

Follow these guidelines:

❖ If the caller does not identify himself or herself, it is proper to ask, "May I say who is calling?" (If you know the individual, greet the person warmly before continuing.)

DON'T RACE TO THE PHONE, OR YOU WILL SOUND AS IF YOU ARE OUT OF BREATH.

❖ Continue, "Just a moment, please."
❖ Place the receiver down quietly and move away before requesting a specific person to come to the phone. Never yell out an individual's name.

What if the person being called is not at home?

*F*or safety reasons, never indicate whether the person is physically present or not. Say, "(Name) is not available to come to the phone right now. May I please take a message?"

See "Taking and Leaving Messages" later in this chapter.

What if someone other than you answers the phone and it is an individual you do not wish to speak with?

*N*ever ask family members to be dishonest by saying, "He's not here." Instead, they should say, "I'm sorry, he is unavailable right now. He will have to call you back later. May I take a message?"

Have a family discussion regarding the ethics and integrity of answering the phone. This issue is important for character building and to the reputation of your family.

How should a housekeeper answer the phone?

*A*n individual working at your home should answer, "Williams residence. Mary Jones speaking." Also, instruct a housekeeper how to take a proper message (as discussed later in this chapter).

NEVER ASK FAMILY MEMBERS TO BE DISHONEST BY SAYING, "HE'S NOT HERE."

PLACING A CALL

What preparation should I make before placing a call?

First, make sure you have the correct number. If you don't have it memorized, write it down. Next, determine the purpose of the call. Other than a social conversation with a close friend, you should never place a call without a reason or objective. Before dialing the number, make a note of the topics you want to cover. Remember, if it is a long distance call, pay attention to the time zone differences.

If no one answers and there is no answering machine, allow the phone to ring approximately seven times before hanging up. It is annoying for a phone to ring and the caller be too impatient to allow the person to answer the phone. If you reach an answering machine, leave a proper message; don't just hang up.

Unless the conversation is purely social, treat every call as a mini-meeting by setting an agenda and deciding what action needs to be taken.

What should be my first words?

Identify yourself immediately. Say "Hello. This is Bill Johnson." Don't expect people to recognize your voice. Never tease, "Guess who this is!"

IF NO ONE ANSWERS AND THERE IS NO ANSWERING MACHINE, ALLOW THE PHONE TO RING APPROXIMATELY SEVEN TIMES BEFORE HANGING UP.

Ask for the person you wish to speak with: "May I please speak to Martha Smith?" Always use first and last names unless you are a personal friend. Never say, "Can I speak with …."

IMPROPER: "Is Martha there?" The person who answers the phone may have to ask, "Martha who?"

PROPER: "Hello. This is Bill Johnson. May I please speak with Martha Smith?"

- ❖ When you have reached the desired party, identify yourself, greet the person warmly, and state the purpose of your call.
- ❖ Never say: "What are you doing?" or "What's happening over there?"
- ❖ Make a habit of asking, "Is this a good time to talk?" If it is not, ask, "When would be a convenient time to call back?"

NOTE: If you know the person who answers the phone, greet that individual warmly before being transferred to the desired party. If you call a number frequently and the same person answers the phone, take the time to engage in a brief, friendly conversation.

What if I reach a wrong number?

*G*et in the habit of dialing slowly and carefully to reach the

*D*ON'T
EXPECT
PEOPLE TO
RECOGNIZE
YOUR
VOICE.

right party. If you don't have the number memorized, be sure it is written down clearly.

If you dial incorrectly and an unexpected voice comes on the line, don't panic! Ask, "Is this 704-867-3167?" If it is not, apologize and say, "I'm sorry. I must have the wrong number." Then end the call. Never slam down the phone.

Should I place a call from another person's phone?

Never make any calls from the phone of your host or hostess without their prior permission. Don't charge long distance calls, even with their permission. People will be polite, even if they resent the charges. Use a credit card or have it billed to your phone number. Also, since dialing an operator for information can be costly, charge those inquiries to your personal billing. Your host should have a directory near every phone. If not, politely ask for one.

How can I help make the call a positive experience?

Give your total attention to the person you have called. Avoid speaking with others in the room and never attempt to multitask or work on another project while you are on the phone.

Practice these rules:

SINCE DIALING AN OPERATOR FOR INFORMATION CAN BE COSTLY, CHARGE THOSE INQUIRIES TO YOUR PERSONAL BILLING.

❖ Refrain from eating or drinking while you are talking. Although the person cannot see you, he can hear you.

❖ Attempt to mentally picture the person with whom you are conversing. It helps give more life to the conversation.

❖ Show continuing interest in the conversation by saying, "Yes" or "I see."

❖ Respond to long answers with an "I agree" or "I'm sorry" along the way.

❖ If you are disconnected, the person placing the call (the host or hostess) should phone back.

Show
continuing
interest in the
conversation
by saying,
"Yes" or
"I see."

ENDING THE CALL

Is there a gracious way to shorten a call? And how should it be concluded?

*I*f you placed the call, it is your responsibility to end the conversation. However, the person you are speaking with may have the "gift of gab" or be an individual who doesn't watch the clock. Here's how you can politely bring the conversation to a conclusion:

❖ Use phrases such as: "Before I must go, let me tell you..." "I know you are busy so I'll let you go."

"Thanks for your time." "Please forgive me, but I have a busy schedule today."

❖ End the call with something positive, such as: "It's always good to talk with you." "Thanks for calling." "It's been fun chatting."

❖ Replace the receiver gently.

The question often arises, "How do I end the call if I have not made the call?"

*I*f you know the person is long-winded, state at the start of the conversation, "I am so glad you called, but I only have a few minutes."

To end the call, take control. Say something such as, "I just looked at my watch and realize we will have to continue this conversation later."

YOUR PHONE VOICE

A phone conversation maybe hidden from view, but you are making a lasting impression. The sound of your voice is extremely important.

Studies have shown that when a person is smiling as he or she speaks, that same warmth comes through the phone. One

THE SOUND OF YOUR VOICE IS EXTREMELY IMPORTANT.

young man actually placed a mirror beside his telephone so he could see himself smile. "It truly changed my attitude on the phone," he exclaimed.

Here are ways to improve the way you sound.

- ❖ Keep the telephone at least one inch from your mouth so that you will not sound garbled.
- ❖ Make sure your volume is neither too loud nor too soft.
- ❖ Speak at a rate slightly slower than normal for greater clarity.
- ❖ Vary your tone and pitch to add vocal variety.
- ❖ Deliberately add energy and excitement to your voice.

One of our cotillion directors told us, "Some callers lift your soul, and others leave you depressed. Some people you look forward to talking with, and some you don't."

What are you communicating to others through your voice and conversation? Perhaps it's time to record a phone call and give yourself an honest self-evaluation.

PERHAPS IT'S TIME TO RECORD A PHONE CALL AND GIVE YOURSELF AN HONEST SELF-EVALUATION.

PROBLEMS TO AVOID

Perhaps you have tried to speak when the radio or television is blaring in the background. Turn down the volume!

Try to eliminate all background noise—whether from people, audio, or poor phone technology. Always apologize to the caller for any extraneous sounds coming through the phone.

Also keep in mind:

❖ Should you need to sneeze or cough, quickly turn your head and cover both your mouth and the phone receiver.

❖ Some phones are equipped with a "mute" button. Learn how to quickly locate this feature and use it as needed.

❖ Don't cradle the phone between your neck and shoulder. It not only distorts your voice, but can eventually cause personal physical damage.

❖ If you must put the receiver down, do so gently.

TAKING AND LEAVING MESSAGES

A great way to keep track of telephone messages is to establish an official family "message center" near the phone in your kitchen. All written phone messages should be posted there, with a space for each member of the household.

Place either notepaper or a Post-it™ pad at every phone in your home. Notes should be taken to the message center immediately.

DON'T CRADLE THE PHONE IN YOUR NECK.

It is helpful to have a telephone directory near every phone. Otherwise you may be absorbing additional charges to obtain numbers from an information operator. Call your phone service provider for extra directories.

The message center should include emergency numbers for police, fire, poison control doctors, and phone numbers for parents at work.

What information is necessary when writing telephone messages?

*N*EVER REPLY WITH IMPATIENCE WHEN YOU ARE ASKED TO TAKE A MESSAGE.

*U*se the "Seven W's" when writing a phone memo:

❖ Who is the message for?
❖ When was the message received? (Date and time)
❖ Who is the message from?
❖ What is the message?
❖ Where should the call be returned? (Phone number)
❖ When is the best time to return the call? (Date and time)
❖ Who took the message?

Be sure to give the caller your full attention. Write clearly and deliver the message without delay.

Never reply with impatience when you are asked to take a message. Sound as if you are delighted with the task. Follow the Golden Rule: If you expect clear, complete messages to be delivered to you, that's how you should prepare them for others.

IMPROPER MESSAGE: Jane called.

PROPER MESSAGE: Mark received a call 4/6 at 6:15 PM from Jane Williams. Can get concert tickets for Friday night. Need to know this evening. Call 704-867-3167 before 10 PM—Mary (person taking call).

What guidelines should I follow when leaving a message?

*A*sk, "Do you have a pen and paper handy?" Then give your first and last name and phone number slowly. Don't hesitate to ask the person to repeat the number.

Do not leave private or personal messages with another person.

Should an R.S.V.P. be answered by telephone?

*A*n invitation to a social event may only be responded to by telephone if a phone number is printed next to the R.S.V.P. Otherwise, you should send a written reply. Be sure to reply promptly.

If you are calling to respond to an invitation, repeat the name of the event, place, date, and time. This is necessary because:

- ❖ The host or hostess needs to know how many guests to plan for.
- ❖ The person extending the invitation needs to be sure the guest knows the location, time, and date of the event.

Do NOT LEAVE PRIVATE OR PERSONAL MESSAGES WITH ANOTHER PERSON.

Is it permissible to leave a response to an R.S.V.P. on an answering machine?

*Y*ou should attempt (at least twice) to speak personally to the person extending the invitation. If unavailable, leave your response on the machine.

ACCEPTING:

IMPROPER RESPONSE: "This is Mary. See you at the picnic!"

PROPER RESPONSE "Hello. This is Mary. I am calling to respond to the invitation to attend the picnic on April 16th from 6 to 9 PM at the Regent Club. Bill and I are looking forward to being with you."

REGRETTING:

IMPROPER RESPONSE: "This is Mary. Got your invitation. Sorry we can't make it."

PROPER RESPONSE: "This is Mary. I am calling to thank you for the invitation to the picnic on April 16th. Unfortunately, we will be unable to attend." If you know the person well, you may give the reason for declining the invitation.

ANSWERING MACHINES

*V*oice mail and electronic answering devices are both a boon and a bane. Owners of such equipment say "It makes my life so much easier." Callers, however, aren't so sure.

The majority of homes have a phone equipped with an answering device to play a pre-recorded personal message when you are unavailable.

NOTE: You should set your answering machine to ring at least five to seven times before playing your greeting. This will give you adequate time to reach the phone.

How can I record the most effective greeting?

*W*e have all listened to greetings that sounded like they were recorded in an echo chamber. Others either shout or speak so softly we can't understand a word.

Always write out your message and practice reading it aloud prior to recording. Here is a recommended greeting for a phone that is used by all members of the family: "Hello. This is the Smith residence. We are unable to answer the phone at this time. Please leave your name and number at the tone and we will return the call as soon as possible."

Avoid saying, "You have reached 704-867-3167," since the caller may have already forgotten your number. Some people are hesitant to give their name, however, callers need to know they have reached the correct residence.

Always write out your message and practice reading it aloud prior to recording.

Never use the pre-recorded message that came with your answering machine. Make it personal. Otherwise, the caller may think they have reached the wrong number.

To make your messages more effective, follow these rules:

❖ Wait at least one second after the beep before starting your greeting.

❖ Move close to the built-in microphone and speak in a normal tone.

❖ Be upbeat! Add some enthusiasm to your voice.

❖ Avoid using music in the background. On a tiny receiver it rarely sounds clear and merely interferes with your message.

❖ Play back your outgoing message. Is it precisely how you want to sound? Do you sound too hurried? Too lifeless and monotonous?

❖ Re-record your greeting until you are satisfied.

How you answer the phone on your machine is just as important as how you would answer in person. You are making a lasting impression.

NOTE: For security reasons, never share your travel plans on an outgoing message. "We'll be on vacation until next Tuesday," is not a smart message to leave.

FOR SECURITY REASONS, NEVER SHARE YOUR TRAVEL PLANS ON AN OUTGOING MESSAGE.

Should I use humor on my recorded message?

*P*erhaps you have dialed a number and heard something like this: "Hi, I'm probably home. I'm just avoiding someone I don't like. Leave me a message and if I don't call back, it's you!"

Unless your profession is comedy and you change your message every day, avoid jokes, humor, and satire on your answering machine. It quickly bores the person who hears it more than once and rarely enhances your image.

NOTE: Don't allow a young child to record your greeting. It is unprofessional and is rarely appreciated by those outside your family.

What rules should I follow when leaving a message?

*S*ome people like to leave a cryptic message such as "It's Bill. Give me a call." The caller assumes you know only one "Bill," and that you know his number. In reality, you may be miles from your phone directory and don't know how to call the person back.

Follow these guidelines:

❖ Keep your message short. Many people set their answering machine to record a maximum of 45 to 60 seconds per message.

❖ Speak clearly and slowly when leaving your message, so people will not need to replay it.

UNLESS YOUR PROFESSION IS COMEDY AND YOU CHANGE YOUR MESSAGE EVERY DAY, AVOID JOKES, HUMOR, AND SATIRE ON YOUR ANSWERING MACHINE.

❖ Avoid leaving jokes or saying, "Guess who this is!" Humor is rarely appreciated in phone messages.

❖ Never say, "This is urgent," unless it truly is.

❖ Leave information concerning only one topic per call. If you have another issue, phone again.

❖ Let people know the best time to call you back.

❖ Always repeat your name and number twice.

❖ Conclude with courtesy—"Thanks," or "Thank you."

IMPROPER: "Hi. This is Judy. Call me about the luncheon."

PROPER: "Hello. This is Judy Smith. I'm calling Sally Jones to remind her about the luncheon at the Hilton at noon on Saturday, May 25th. Please return my call at 890-098-7890. Again, this is Judy Smith at 890-098-7890. Thank you."

How can I keep up with the large number of incoming messages?

*D*on't allow your messages to pile up. Check your phone several times each day—even if that means access from a remote location.

❖ Keep a pad and paper handy to note phone numbers and any action you must take.

❖ Delete answering machine messages immediately after listening.

❖ Only save a message that contains details someone else needs to hear.

KEEP A PAD AND PAPER HANDY TO NOTE PHONE NUMBERS AND ANY ACTION YOU MUST TAKE.

NOTE: Set your phone to ring at least five to seven times to give you a chance to answer the phone (if you choose to).

VOICE MAIL

*I*f you need an answering system with far more options than an answering machine, subscribe to voice mail. It will greatly expand your ability to manage incoming and outgoing messages.

Many homes utilize a multibox voice mail system, one mailbox for each member of the family. Unfortunately, some people use the system as their first line of communication. Don't fall into that trap. Remember, everyone would rather speak person to person.

What is the most convenient manner of handling incoming voice mail messages?

*F*ollow the motto of the Boy Scouts: "Be Prepared."

Always have a pen and notepad handy to take notes. This is especially important regarding any follow-up action that may be necessary.

   ❖   Be sure to listen to the entire message. If you assume that you know what the person is about to say, you may be wrong. Far too often people think, "I know

IF YOU ASSUME THAT YOU KNOW WHAT THE PERSON IS ABOUT TO SAY, YOU MAY BE WRONG.

what he is going to say," and delete the message halfway through.

❖ Check and clear your voice mail at least twice each day.

❖ Do not allow a message to remain on your voice mail for more than 24 hours.

Since leaving and retrieving electronic messages via voice mail and other devices will most likely be a part of your life forever, don't forget your manners in the digital world.

CALL WAITING

In our opinion, possibly no other electronic device has caused so much ill-mannered behavior as Call Waiting. This is the service you subscribe to that emits a beep when someone is attempting to phone you while you are on another call. What's the result? You interrupt your conversation to find out who is trying to reach you. And, by doing so, you are implying to the first caller, "This incoming call is more important than you."

Should I ignore the Call Waiting signal?

Only use this service when you are expecting an urgent call. The person you are speaking with is your priority, not another caller.

Do not allow a message to remain on your voice mail for more than 24 hours.

If you do use Call Waiting:

❖ At the start of the conversation, tell the caller, "I'm expecting a call from John Brown. If I have to leave the line for a moment, please excuse me."

❖ Always apologize to the original caller for an interruption.

❖ Make it a policy that you will rarely place your friends on hold.

❖ Never say, "I just received a very important call. I need to go now." That's impolite.

❖ If you are not expecting an urgent call, ignore the beep.

CALLER ID

*M*illions of phones are equipped with Caller ID, a service that allows you to see the phone number (and in many areas, the name) of the person dialing. Many people use it to screen their calls.

Some callers are surprised when they call and the first words are, "Hi, George!"

"How did you know it was me?" the caller responds.

"It says so right on my phone."

When using Caller ID, follow these rules:

MAKE IT A POLICY THAT YOU WILL RARELY PLACE YOUR FRIENDS ON HOLD.

- ❖ If you do not wish to speak to the person, let it go to your answering machine or voice mail after three rings. However, always return a call when requested to.
- ❖ Answer your phone with "Hello. This is (your full name)."
- ❖ Don't brag about your ID program to the caller.

Remember, some people have devices that automatically reject all calls from those who have blocked their Caller ID. Know your phone's code for unblocking the system.

Don't brag about your ID program to the caller.

Telephone Rules to Remember

After discussing the contents of this chapter with members of your family, decide how your home phone will be used. The four most important concerns are:

- ❖ Set the hours and situations when you should and should not place or receive calls.
- ❖ Determine the maximum length of time for calls.
- ❖ Establish a specific style for receiving and placing calls.
- ❖ Have an official message-taking system.

NOTE: Chapter Seven includes phone rules for children.

RESPONDING TO SOLICITORS

Is there a polite way of dealing with unwanted phone solicitations?

*L*aws allow certain nonprofit organizations and companies you have previously done business with to call your number. While you may not be interested in what they have to offer, treat them with kindness and avoid being rude. There is no reason to become angry or upset—it only results in interrupting your day.

Without being harsh or unkind, simply say, "Thanks for your call, but I'm not interested," then conclude the conversation.

Or, you may respond, "Would you please remove my name from your list? Thank you so much."

If the caller continues to talk, repeat the above response. Then politely conclude the call.

THERE IS NO REASON TO BECOME ANGRY OR UPSET—IT ONLY RESULTS IN INTERRUPTING YOUR DAY.

COMPUTER COURTESIES

*W*ith surprising speed, the computer has become an activity center in millions of homes. It is a source for news, business, entertainment, an educational treasure trove, and the portal through which we view the world and keep in touch with our friends. However, like any valuable resource, sensible guidelines for its use need to be established.

What limits should be placed on the use of a home computer by family members?

Computers can become addictive. Without realizing why, some individuals find themselves spending hundreds of hours every month glued to the monitor—chatting with friends, playing online games, or uncovering facts about their field of interest.

One father confessed, "We finally had to have a discussion and limit the use of the computer for family members. Otherwise, we would never have time for conversation."

Follow these guidelines:

❖ Like the phone, computer use (especially for chatting with friends) should be limited to fifteen minutes.

❖ The computer should be a family resource, not dominated by one individual.

❖ Turn the monitor off during meals and other specified times.

❖ The audio volume should be kept low and not be allowed to interfere with others who may be nearby.

Turn the monitor off during meals and other specified times.

Where should the home computer be located?

*T*he computer should be located in either the family room or the home office. Make sure the computer screen faces the center of the room. And, since parents should always monitor Internet use, do not place a computer in the bedroom of a child.

NOTE: If you are using a dial-up Internet connection as oppposed to wireless, have a separate phone line for your Internet service, or purchase a piece of equipment that sends an incoming call to voice mail. It is frustrating to hear a busy signal for hours when someone ties up the phone line with a computer.

Later, in Chapter Seven, we will discuss how parents can help ensure that their children have a positive computer experience.

TELEVISION ETIQUETTE

A study reported by the American Family Research Council found that parents spend less than 40 minutes each week in meaningful conversation with their children. Why such a small amount of time? The answer is found in one word: television.

The average child spends four hours every day watching television—and from birth to the age of 18 spends more time in front of a television set than in the classroom.

SINCE PARENTS SHOULD ALWAYS MONITOR INTERNET USE, DO NOT PLACE A COMPUTER IN THE BEDROOM OF A CHILD.

Instead of allowing televison to dominate your home life, take a proactive approach. For example, decide in advance what programs you will watch as a family each evening, and limit the number of hours the set is in use.

Where should television sets be located in the home?

Ideally, the television should be located in the family room. You may want additional sets in the kitchen and master bedroom.

We highly discourage placing a television in the bedroom of any child—even during the teen years. It not only isolates children from the family, but makes it almost impossible to monitor viewing habits. Plus, the television can interfere with both study time and sleep.

For those occasions when your children are having a sleep-over and want to watch a movie in their room, use a portable set equipped with a DVD player.

How can television become a more positive influence on our family?

Television is for either information or relaxation, and only you can decide how it should be used.

A family in South Carolina uses television news as a catalyst for family discussions. Said the mother, "At least one evening each

WE HIGHLY DISCOURAGE PLACING A TELEVISION IN THE BEDROOM OF ANY CHILD— EVEN DURING THE TEEN YEARS.

week we watch a thirty-minute local newscast together. Then we turn off the set and spend another half hour discussing the day's local and national issues—even sports."

Many families decide in advance what programs they will watch. This is a wise move, since the Center for Media Education states, "By the time children complete elementary school, the average child will witness more than 100,000 acts of violence on TV, including 8,000 murders."

To help make television watching a more positive experience, we recommend these rules:

- ❖ Don't turn on the television during mealtimes. It is an unnecessary distraction and takes away from family conversation.
- ❖ When watching, keep comments to a minimum so as not to disturb others. Wait until a commercial break to offer your opinions or questions.
- ❖ No member of the family should be allowed to "channel surf" when others are watching, unless, of course, permission is asked.
- ❖ Practice proper seating habits. For example, one person should not be allowed to "stretch out" on a sofa and deny seating to others.

Remember, television viewing is a family activity—and every member of your household is equally important.

Remember, television viewing is a family activity—and every member of your household is equally important.

What television courtesies should be observed when guests are visiting our home?

*I*f you invite friends to your home and are planning to watch a particular television program or movie, let them know in advance. They should accept or decline the invitation based on that information.

When guests enter the home, all family members should rise—even those who are watching a television program. It is also polite to turn off the set when friends arrive.

If you are a guest and wish to carry on a conversation with a particular family member, ask that person to leave the room. Don't disturb others.

What etiquette issues involve electronic equipment?

*F*or reasons of economics and safety, turn off the television set when not in use. If the monitor is in a cabinet, close the doors when not in use.

We recommend having a policy that you will not borrow or loan electronic equipment. Unforeseen problems may arise that can cause ill will between friends. It's better to give a piece of used equipment than to loan it.

NOTE: When you check out media from a library or retail store, treat it with respect. Always replace it in the proper container and return before the due date.

*I*T'S BETTER TO GIVE A PIECE OF USED EQUIPMENT THAN TO LOAN IT.

MUSIC MANNERS

A gentleman in Atlanta loved opera music so much that he piped it through a loudspeaker system around the swimming pool in his backyard. There was only one problem. He turned up the volume so loud the neighbors two blocks away could hear it!

Soon there was a knock on the door from the local police. "What's wrong?" he wanted to know.

"Sir, if you don't turn down the volume, we will have to fine you for disturbing the peace."

What rules should be established for music at home?

*J*ust because one member of your household enjoys a certain type of music doesn't mean that others must be subjected to it day and night. That's why it is important to form a consensus regarding when, where, and how music is to be played in your home.

Here are guidelines worth adopting:

- ❖ The audio from Internet, radio, television, or CDs should not be blasted throughout the home.
- ❖ The music volume should never interfere with normal conversation.

IT IS IMPORTANT TO FORM A CONSENSUS REGARDING WHEN, WHERE, AND HOW MUSIC IS TO BE PLAYED IN YOUR HOME.

CHILDREN AND TEENS SHOULD NOT BE ALLOWED TO WEAR STEREO HEADSETS AT MEAL TIMES OR DURING OTHER FAMILY ACTIVITIES.

❖ If possible, earbuds should be used with audio devices such as the computer, video games, iPods, and other handheld electronics. Remember that even when using earbuds, the volume should never be audible to those around you.

❖ Children and teens should not be allowed to wear stereo headsets at meal times or during other family activities.

❖ Specific time limits should be placed on children's music listening habits so that they will not interfere with homework or sleep.

Later in this book we will address the issue of music in public places and recommend specific guidelines for parents.

$\mathcal{T}$ODAY'S NETIQUETTE

$\mathcal{T}$he rules of common courtesy apply to every form of communication—whether it be in person, wired, or wireless. Internet and e-mail users are certainly not immune. They've even coined a phrase for online etiquette—netiquette.

From e-mail to Instant Messaging and "tweeting," here are the principles and practices that will guide you to what is proper and acceptable when exchanging messages in cyberspace.

E-MAIL

$\mathcal{S}$ending and receiving e-mail is no longer a novelty. It has become a primary means of communication for friends, families, and businesses. In the workplace, it has virtually replaced the interoffice memo.

Still, we need to ask: Is e-mail the most appropriate form for this message? Or should I send a fax or regular letter? For example, e-mail is not appropriate for:

❖ Sending or responding to formal invitations.

❖ A letter of condolence.

❖ A "thank you" letter for a gift or kindness.

❖ A formal contract, document, or agreement.

A written response (whether typed or handwritten) conveys greater importance and is more highly valued than an e-mail.

What are the basic rules for preparing an e-mail?

*T*he key to effective e-mail is to communicate simply and directly. People don't expect you to be an experienced writer, but they do want you to follow the rules.

Your letter should get to the point quickly and stick with the subject—don't wander. You should not have more than one or two topics in your e-mail.

Here are the basic guidelines to follow:

❖ If the message is informal, write casually. If it is serious, pay close attention to your word usage and grammar.

❖ Short paragraphs are better than long ones.

❖ An e-mail is not a telegram. Write in complete sentences.

❖ Do not write in all lowercase (or all uppercase) letters.

❖ Avoid the overuse of punctuation. Let your words provide the emphasis.

LET YOUR WORDS PROVIDE THE EMPHASIS.

- ❖ If you are asking for a decision, include enough data for an appropriate response.
- ❖ Be careful about using satire or irony. The reader can't see your facial expressions, only your words.

Be specific about dates and times. Avoid saying "tomorrow" or "next Friday." You can't be certain when the e-mail will be read. Write "Friday, June 28 at 3 PM." Also, write the month as a word, not a number. In the U.S. 7/3/06 is July 3rd. In Europe the first two numbers are reversed so it would read as March 7th.

Your e-mail should convey the same courtesy used in everyday conversation. Remind yourself to say "thank you" and "please." Always use good taste and show respect for others.

Always use good taste and show respect for others.

What technical issues should I be concerned with?

Stick to the basic ASCII (American Standard Code for Information Interchange) format used by nearly all e-mail programs. Other configurations may convert into gibberish. And limit the length of your lines to fewer than eighty characters. Otherwise, the recipient may see strange formatting and line breaks.

Remember these rules:

- ❖ Don't indent or use tabs since the receiver may not have the same format. Instead, add a line space and start the new paragraph flush left.

- ❖ Avoid using text art, color type, or special backgrounds as part of your e-mail. The recipient's program may not be able to download them.
- ❖ Never type in all uppercase letters. People will think you are shouting—plus, it is very difficult to read.
- ❖ Double check your grammar and spelling. If your e-mail program does not have a spellcheck, type the message in a word processor, check it, then copy to your e-mail program.
- ❖ Always read every word you type before you press the "send" button.

NEVER LEAVE A SUBJECT LINE BLANK.

NOTE: Double check the name you are entering from your address book. An e-mail sent to the person above or below the entry could be quite embarrassing.

What should be included in the subject line?

Every e-mail should include a subject line. Never leave it blank. And make sure the subject accurately conveys the content of the message you are sending.

Avoid attention-getting symbols such as "<<<<<<<READ THIS NOW>>>>>>>>>>" or !!!!!!!! WOW! !!!!!!!! Some people will think this is a commercial message, or will consider you quite immature.

PROPER SUBJECT LINE: Requested Netiquette Guidelines

What are the guidelines for sending to multiple recipients?

*K*eep your target list rather short, and review your "CC:" list regularly to add or delete names. Also, avoid sending e-mail to people who may not be interested.

NOTE: If you are sending messages to a large list of individuals who don't know each other, use BCC (blind carbon copy). This will avoid your entire receiving list appearing on the message. When you use BCC, the recipient will see only his or her name and yours.

When is it appropriate to add a file attachment?

*A*void sending unsolicited attachments. Because of fear of receiving a possible computer virus, some people never open them. Consider sending an e-mail in advance asking if the person would like to receive the attachment.

Only attach files if they are essential. They take time to download, use considerable memory on someone's computer, and often don't convert to the user's word processing program.

Also, when you receive an attachment, don't download it without running an antivirus program. (Make sure a

Avoid sending e-mail to people who may not be interested.

permanent antivirus program is running on your computer at all times.)

What is considered a proper "signature" for my e-mail?

*Y*our signature is the information at the close of an e-mail and contains important data.

❖ Keep your signature short—three or four lines maximum.
❖ Include your full name, address, phone, fax, e-mail, and any alternative means of reaching you.
❖ If you use a quote or humorous phrase as part of your signature, keep the item short—and be sure no one may be offended by it.
❖ Change clever sayings often. After several e-mails they are no longer amusing.

IMPROPER SIGNATURE: National League of Cotillions "Always treat others with honor, dignity, and respect."

PROPER SIGNATURE: National League of Cotillions Mail: P.O. Box 204384, Charlotte, NC 28224 Phone: 1-800-633-7947 Fax: 1-704-864-3232 E-mail: cotillions@nljc.com Internet: www.nljc.com

Also, try to avoid signatures that build a picture out of keyboard characters. They usually become mangled on someone else's system.

What guidelines should be observed when replying to an e-mail message?

Make it a personal rule that you will not reply to an original message more than once. When you keep adding comments to the "thread" the message can become confusing.

Some e-mails also have files attached which can take up precious memory space. It is better to send a new e-mail than to resend extremely long or multiple messages.

Here are additional rules for replying:

❖ Respond as soon as possible to the e-mail messages you receive.

❖ Change the subject line to match your reply.

❖ Some people send so many e-mails, they may not remember the content of what they sent. Always refer to the most important issue of the original message as a reminder to the sender in your reply.

❖ If the person has spent considerable time sending you a message, it is discourteous to give a curt reply such as "Ditto," or "I agree." Write at least one or two full paragraphs.

ALWAYS REFER TO THE MOST IMPORTANT ISSUE OF THE ORIGINAL MESSAGE AS A REMINDER TO THE SENDER IN YOUR REPLY.

❖ Never respond quickly to an e-mail that upsets you. If you feel annoyed or angry, wait at least one day to reply.

Also, do not reply to an entire list unless your answer is of interest (and applies) to all. And don't edit a quoted message. The meaning could be changed and the original writer could be offended.

NOTE: When you receive an important e-mail, give a quick response that it has been received—and let the person know approximately when you will be replying. If your computer crashes, don't use this as an excuse for not communicating. Reply instead by phone, fax, or overnight letter.

IF YOUR COMPUTER CRASHES, DON'T USE THIS AS AN EXCUSE FOR NOT COMMUNICATING.

What are the rules regarding the forwarding of e-mail?

You should not forward an e-mail without the permission of the original sender. And if you only forward a portion of an email, add a note to explain what you have done.

For privacy reasons, always delete the distribution list before forwarding.

Here's a word of caution: Never be tempted to forward a get-rich-quick scheme, a conspiracy theory, or a chain letter.

Should I be concerned with e-mail privacy?

$\mathcal{A}$ssume the e-mail administrators of your web server have the ability to read your messages—because they do! And be aware that many companies monitor the e-mail messages of their employees, and assume they may read yours.

Also, remember that it is possible for "hackers" to read your e-mail. Some people do it for fun.

Finally, never include your personal or business credit card number in an e-mail message.

What is meant by an e-mail "flame"?

In the invisible electronic world, some people become upset when your etiquette does not meet their standards. They may even respond by sending a rather hot message—called a "flame."

Who can expect a negative response?

❖ The person who writes in ALL CAPS. You'll be accused of "SHOUTING."
❖ The sender of an unsolicited mass mailing.
❖ The person who makes a comment about someone's grammar, spelling, or punctuation.

What should you do if you receive such a reply? If it is from someone you don't know, ignore it. You don't want to get into a "flame war." If it comes from a friend, reply and apologize if necessary.

$\mathcal{N}$EVER INCLUDE YOUR PERSONAL OR BUSINESS CREDIT CARD NUMBER IN AN E-MAIL MESSAGE.

How should I handle unsolicited "spam" e-mail?

It is futile to become upset and attempt to contact the sender. Instead, discuss the matter with your Internet service provider. They will help you install an anti-spam filter. The same advice applies to "pop-up" advertising that is an invasion of your privacy. Free programs such as POP-UP STOPPER (www.panicware.com) are excellent for reducing the problem.

INSTANT MESSAGING

Without question, the preferred choice of distance communication among teens is Instant Messaging (IM)—which comes in many forms and from a variety of sources. It has spread to millions of older users worldwide.

People like it because it's lightning quick. The questions and answers are exchanged in "real time" and you are actually in a real conversation.

While e-mail is great for sending memos and files, IM is best for short messages and fast responses. There are many benefits:

❖ You are in control of who you converse with.
❖ You can set your online schedule.
❖ It's possible to take a break. You can't do that during a phone call.

WHILE E-MAIL IS GREAT FOR SENDING MEMOS AND FILES, IM IS BEST FOR SHORT MESSAGES AND FAST RESPONSES.

❖ It allows you to keep in touch with your friends and relatives.

❖ You can talk and do several other computer-related tasks at once.

❖ You can engage in multiple conversations at the same time.

❖ It decreases phone bills for those who communicate over a distance.

What courtesies should I observe when working with my "buddy list"?

With AOL's Instant Messenger software, Yahoo!, Microsoft's MSN Messenger, and other programs, you set up a contact list or "buddy list" of those with whom you frequently communicate. From the names you can see who is online. It also helps create a safe environment.

Some individuals have more than one hundred people entered on their list. Your "buddy" directory should not be used to make new friends, but to keep in contact with those you have.

Your "BUDDY" DIRECTORY SHOULD NOT BE USED TO MAKE NEW FRIENDS, BUT TO KEEP IN CONTACT WITH THOSE YOU HAVE.

❖ Be truthful. If you click the icons "Available" or "Online," make certain you really are. Also, if you click "Busy" or "Do not disturb," that should also be the fact.

❖ If someone is marked "Away," don't pester him or her.

❖ Allow a person offline time to respond. He or she may want to talk later.

❖ If you are sending messages across the country, know the time zones. Don't message when a person is sleeping or having meals.

What's the best way to start and end messages?

$\mathcal{B}$egin by requesting the person's time. "Do you have a minute?" "Can we chat?" or, "Are you busy?" End with, "I need to sign off," or, "That's it for now."

What are the benefits of Instant Messaging in the business environment?

$\mathcal{T}$he number of corporations and small businesses using this form of communication continues to grow. Why?

❖ It is an ideal way for a group of people in different locations who are working on the same task to communicate.

❖ Organizations find it an inexpensive way to stay in touch with staff that are on the road.

❖ It's great for informal communications. (Avoid using IM for formal requests, since it lacks an aura of significance.)

$\mathcal{D}$ON'T MESSAGE WHEN A PERSON IS SLEEPING OR HAVING MEALS.

What concerns should I have about sending picture messages?

*M*ost cell phones allow you to add a written message below a photo you are sending (check "Options"). Or, you can attach an audio note to the picture. Be careful of what you write or say, since the recipient may share it with friends. For example, never make a snide or critical remark of anyone in the photo.

TWITTER ETIQUETTE

*M*illions are staying in touch and following their friends on twitter.com with short 140-character messages as they "tweet."

Here are a few guidelines:

- ❖ Let each tweet stand on its own as a complete sentence rather than, "Yeah, I know."
- ❖ Make sure you look at a tweeter's profile before following them.
- ❖ Don't use too many acronyms.
- ❖ Be careful where you tweet. It's out of place at solemn occasions such as funerals, court hearings, etc.
- ❖ Don't be a spoiler. Avoid sharing the ending of a movie or even a televised sporting event someone may be recording for later playback.

Be careful where you tweet. It's out of place at solemn occasions such as funerals, court hearings, etc.

❖ Avoid over-promoting yourself or a product.

❖ Remember, what you tweet is public and can impact your reputation.

ABBREVIATIONS AND SYMBOLS

*N*etiquette has developed its own unique codes of communication. The abbreviations and symbols below are sometimes used in informal e-mail between friends and family.

We present this list to help you understand some of the messages you may receive, not as a recommendation for your writing style.

I've seen a few typographical symbols on my e-mails. What do they mean?

*S*ome writers use a few keystrokes to create "smileys." Since they express human emotion, others call them "emoticons." If you turn your head to the left you will see the face of the smiley. These symbols are usually placed at the end of a sentence and refer to what's been said.

Also, placing the "greater-smaller" keystrokes around a word can indicate emotion: <sigh> <grin>.

We recommend you use these symbols sparingly—or not at all. To most people, they are signs of a new e-mail writer,

*A*VOID OVER-PROMOTING YOURSELF OR A PRODUCT.

or someone trying to be humorous. Whenever possible, convey your thoughts with words, not symbols.

How can I emphasize words when there is no underline keystroke available?

*H*ere's how many e-mail users solve the problem. To emphasize a word or a phrase, surround it with "stars." Example: "I *warned* you not to tell her!"

Also, since e-mail does not have an underlining feature, you can surround your type with the underscore symbol to indicate it: Example: _Gone_with_ the_Wind_. Some writers use hyphens: Gone-with-the-Wind.

The style in which you communicate with e-mail and Instant Messaging is a reflection of your character and personality. Make certain you treat your unseen friends with admiration and respect.

FACEBOOK AND MYSPACE ETIQUETTE

*S*ocial networks took a giant leap forward when Facebook burst on the scene in 2004. MySpace was launched in 2003. Instagram was released in 2010. These networks attract hundreds of millions of users. As of 2014, Facebook reports over 1.28 billion monthly active users.

To EMPHASIZE A WORD OR A PHRASE, SURROUND IT WITH "STARS."

Never arrange to personally meet someone who contacts you through a social media site without a trusted friend present.

People use social networks to enter a personal profile, connect with existing friends and acquaintances, find new or mutual friends, and share information, pictures, videos, and articles with others. The use of these tools has revolutionized what it means to "connect." Before the era of social networking, to reconnect with a friend might mean a quick phone call, an email, or a lunch date. Now, it is possible to know exactly what is going on in a friend's life without ever even speaking to him or her. Consider the implications of this "virtual" connection on society. When one used to pick up the phone and call a friend to catch up, it is now possible to obtain a considerable amount of information without investing any more time than is required to type a name. While it is convenient to remain in contact with others without the need to pick up the phone or plan a visit, consistently choosing "quick and easy" forms of connection over real, personal contact (such as enjoying a meal, walk, or quiet phone call with a friend) can result in maintaining many shallow, surface-level relationships and very few real, meaningful ones. Often, Facebook users report increased feelings of loneliness and isolation after browsing the network. This goes to show that not all forms of connectedness make us feel truly connected.

That said, social networks allow users a platform for building further connections and can be used in a responsible and healthy way to grow a meaningful personal network. Remember to use social networks to supplement, but not replace, your "real" networks.

FACEBOOK

*W*ithout question, the preferred social media tool for teenagers and most adults is Facebook. Over 1.28 billion people use Facebook on a monthly basis. Facebook includes a public profile, private "chat" messages, and both public and private photo albums. Facebook is a great tool for reconnecting with friends, classmates, colleagues, and relatives. There are many benefits to establishing and maintaining an account:

❖ Facebook allows users to organize social events quickly and easily and maintain up-to-date communication with event-goers.

❖ One can connect with a new acquaintance with ease by adding that contact as a "friend."

❖ Social networking may help you maintain a friendship that would have otherwise dissolved due to distance or other separating factors.

❖ Facebook includes a messenger application that allows instant communication between users and file and data sharing. In many ways, this can be useful for casual conversation and discussion. For more information regarding instant messaging, refer to the guidelines beginning on page 62.

FACEBOOK IS A GREAT TOOL FOR RECONNECTING WITH FRIENDS, CLASSMATES, COLLEAGUES, AND RELATIVES.

What guidelines should I follow while using Facebook?

❖ Assume everything you post online to be public information. While settings may allow certain posts to remain "private," it is best to err on the safe side and refrain from posting anything, whether it may be a photograph, message, or comment, that would reflect poorly on your person if it were to become "public" information. This includes negative comments or "wall posts," inappropriate photographs (see list below), or private personal information (even if in a private chat message). While some level of privacy is implied, it is important to remember that with any type of internet or computer network, it is possible for others to obtain your password and access your postings and information, so it is best to avoid posting anything you would not want anyone (and everyone) the ability to access.

❖ Carefully monitor use of any social network by children (specifically, minors under eighteen years of age). Parents, consider requiring children (or minors living in your home) to provide you with access to their account for monitoring. A child will be less likely to post inappropriate information if a parent has access. "Privacy" is a privilege reserved for adults and those not legally dependent upon a guardian and should not be used to defend inappropriate Internet use by children. Young children should not be allowed access to social networking unless all content to be posted is reviewed and approved by a parent or guardian.

❖ Educate your children about online predators and tactics that might be used against them to obtain personal information.

❖ Encourage children to consider their goals and ambitions before allowing the use of social networks. A good rule to use when deciding whether or not to post a picture, statement, or message on a Facebook account is to ask, "If I were to run for president or political office some day, would it hurt my campaign if this information were released to the public?" This simple question should help you determine whether your comment or photograph is acceptable to share online. For more information on parental monitoring of social network use, see chapter 7 (Parent's Guide to Electronic Etiquette).

❖ Never arrange to personally meet someone who contacts you through a social media site without a trusted friend present. This applies to "online dating" especially. Sexual predators often use social networks to ensnare victims.

REMEMBER, EVERYTHING SHARED ON A SOCIAL NETWORKING SITE IS A DIRECT REFLECTION OF YOUR CHARACTER.

❖ Remember, everything shared on a social network is a direct reflection of your character. Choose to "share yourself" in the very best light!

What courtesies should be observed when using a Facebook account?

❖ Respond promptly to event requests and invitations. Consider an event request similar to a mailed invitation and respond as quickly as you are able. Likewise, if you receive a message that requires a response, either choose to respond in a timely manner or contact the friend directly and let him/her know you do not use Facebook frequently but would love to speak with him/her directly regarding the message.

❖ When messaging a friend via Facebook, avoid asking personal questions or sharing another's personal information. There is nothing worse than having a friend post an embarrassing comment for the world to see.

❖ Consider utilizing the privacy setting that allows users to approve all comments and postings before they are visible to the public. This will prevent inappropriate posts from being shared on your personal "wall" without your knowledge.

Avoid asking personal questions on sharing another's personal information.

❖ Maintain an accurate and up-to-date profile. If you choose to share personal information by creating a public profile, keep it updated.

❖ Use proper grammar whenever possible. Abbreviations may be convenient at times, but they can cause ambiguities or misunderstandings that could easily be avoided by simply using correct speech.

❖ If you notice an acquaintance posting inappropriate comments, photographs, etc. frequently, consider removing them from your contacts/friends list. Remember, those with whom you associate reflect on your character, and Facebook is no exception to this rule.

Ask: IS THIS PHOTOGRAPH A POSITIVE REPRESENTATION OF THOSE PICTURED?

INSTAGRAM

Instagram is an application that allows users to take and share photographs and videos on various social networks. It is gaining popularity since being acquired by Facebook in 2012 and has a quite large user base. Currently, it is estimated there are 100 million active users. Carefully consider the following when posting a photograph to Instagram, or any other form of social media account:

Activate Privacy Settings That Require Approval Of Followers.

Before posting a photograph to a social network, ask:

❖ Is this photograph a positive representation of those pictured (self included?)

❖ Would you, or anyone else, be embarrassed if the photo were to become "public"?

❖ Is everyone in the photograph dressed appropriately?

❖ Does this photograph portray you or others engaging in excessive alcohol or illicit drug use? If so, refrain from sharing this photograph.

❖ Does this photograph share more personal information than would be appropriate? For example, avoid posting pictures of an invitation to another's party that includes an address or phone number.

❖ Activate privacy settings that require approval of followers. This will enable you to select and filter who can see your feed of photos and videos. Also, use caution when choosing to include the location of your photos. This can be a safety concern, especially if you do not have privacy settings preventing unknown followers. It is best to require approval of all followers and refrain from posting the location of your photos unless you intend for others to know where the photo was taken.

YOUTUBE PROTOCOL

Every day, thousands of short video clips are downloaded and shown on YouTube, a site owned by Google. Some videos are seen by millions of Internet users.

While it is tempting to create a wild or crazy video of yourself, you need to consider the bigger picture. What if, a few years from now, you send your resumé to a large corporation and they do an Internet search as part of their due diligence and up comes an offensive video with you as the star? Well, there goes your job!

You may say, "Well I had that deleted." Good luck! Virtually everything you have ever posted on the Internet is still on someone's hard drive—and it can be retrieved. This includes what you have posted on Facebook, MySpace, YouTube, and every e-mail you have ever written.

This is why you need to treat yourself and others with honor, dignity, and respect.

LINKEDIN DO'S AND DON'TS

What Facebook and MySpace are to the nonprofessional, LinkedIn is to the world of those in business and commerce.

Today, over 50 million professionals use LinkedIn to exchange information, ideas, and opportunities.

Today, over 50 million professionals use it to exchange information, ideas, and opportunities.

Here are a few recommendations when using this site:

CONGRATULATE OTHERS ON A NEW JOB OR PROMOTION.

THE DO'S

❖ Do update your profile regularly.

❖ Do join groups selectively.

❖ Do go on the offensive (get rid of digital dirt: review sites and personal blogs you are linked to).

❖ Do write honest and valuable recommendations.

❖ Do grow your network by joining industry and alumni groups related to your business.

❖ Do congratulate others on a new job or promotion.

THE DON'TS

❖ Don't badmouth a current or previous employer.

❖ Don't forget others can see your friends.

❖ Don't let connection requests sit for too long.

❖ Don't upload a nonprofessional headshot.

❖ Don't use status updates to share personal details (save that for Facebook).

❖ Don't join groups that dishonor another group, race, or ethnicity.

❖ Don't forget that first impressions are lasting, and potential clients may research your name.

The messages you send into cyberspace are not to be taken lightly. They become part of your reputation and can greatly affect your future.

FOUR

Electronic Etiquette at the Office

How times have changed! In the early 1900s there were only two or three telephones for every one hundred people—and that included businesses.

It didn't make any difference whether you managed the local bank, ran the hardware store, or lived on a farm: the only way to make a call was to walk up to a wall-mounted wooden box, lift the receiver, and hope no one else was talking. If all was clear, you would wind the crank to get the attention of the operator at the central phone office.

There was absolutely no privacy. Every line was shared with at least eight parties, and you could listen in on conversations anytime you wanted.

Yet, even then phone etiquette was important. In 1914, the telephone company in Elkhorn, Wisconsin, published these guidelines for its 600 subscribers:

- ❖ Calls are limited to three minutes.
- ❖ No party should hold the line for longer than five minutes.
- ❖ Don't waste the operator's time in useless talk.

❖ If you will "ring off," the operator will not have to listen to know when you are through.

Just imagine conducting business on the phone under those circumstances!

Today, the number of telephones numbers in the billions. And without the ability of instant communication, world business would come to a grinding halt.

Here's a guide to telephone etiquette and manners in today's workplace.

ANSWERING THE BUSINESS PHONE

The manager of a computer warehouse called his office when he was out of the city and was shocked when the receptionist answered abruptly, "Hang on! I'm placing you on hold!"

There was no, "Good afternoon. This is Mary. How can I help you?"

The manager was tempted to give the employee an instant lecture, but instead he called a staff meeting the next day and set the rules for how company phones were to be answered.

The first voice heard by a caller becomes the image of the organization. Since first impressions are lasting, it is extremely important that the person chosen to answer the phone is personable, well-trained, and professional.

THE FIRST VOICE HEARD BY A CALLER BECOMES THE IMAGE OF THE ORGANIZATION.

Regardless of the size of your organization and the complexity of the communication system, there are three basics we should never forget:

❖ Every caller should be treated with sincere courtesy and respect.
❖ Callers should be connected to a real person as quickly as possible, not subjected to a maze of voice message choices.
❖ The requests of every caller should be met.

Now let's look at the ways these objectives are accomplished.

How should a receptionist or secretary properly answer the office phone?

Immediately, in a positive, professional tone, say "Good morning, National League of Cotillions, Hannah speaking. How may I help you?"

Be as polite and helpful as possible. If the caller asks, "I'd like to speak with Mr. Winters," respond with, "May I tell him who is calling please?" If you do not recognize the caller, inquire: "May I ask what this pertains to?"

Never tell the caller, "He's out for coffee," or "He is at the doctor's office." This is personal information people do not need

Every caller should be treated with sincere courtesy and respect.

to know. If the individual is out of the office, say so before asking who is calling. Don't give the impression you are screening calls.

Should the person being called be an available, say, "Would you like for me to transfer you to his (or her) voice mail, or would you like for me to take a message?" Often, the caller will prefer that you create a handwritten message (see "Taking and Leaving Messages" in Chapter Two).

How should employees in various departments receive a call?

It is best to answer by giving your full name—and even your department. "Hello, this is Customer Relations, John Morgan speaking." Use your name, but not your title.

If your message is on voice mail, say: "You've reached the voice mail of John Morgan in Customer Relations. Please leave your message and phone number. I will return your call as soon as possible. Thank you." Make sure your tone is warm and friendly.

How should I respond if an important call arrives while I have a visitor in my office?

Your guest should always take priority. If the call is of an emergency nature, ask the guest to remain in your office while you go to another location. Keep the phone conversation short and return as quickly as possible.

"Hello, this is Customer Relations, John Morgan speaking." Use your name, but not your title.

If you are the guest when such a call comes in, offer to exit the room so the person can have privacy. Should you be asked to remain, direct your attention to something else while the person completes the call.

What are the guidelines for answering someone's office phone?

*T*here may be times you are requested to take calls for someone else. When that happens:

- ❖ Answer by saying, "Bob Smith's line, Jim Brown speaking."
- ❖ Explain the reason you are answering the phone.
- ❖ Don't make a promise that the person will call back. You can only say, "Thank you. I will give him the message."
- ❖ Be careful when speaking about a colleague. Avoid saying, "He's in the restroom," or "She is still having lunch."

How can I avoid spending too much time receiving calls?

*I*f you're not careful, the telephone can dominate your schedule. Here are ways to avoid that trap:

- ❖ Have frequent discussions with your receptionist or secretary regarding how you want your calls screened.

*B*E CAREFUL WHEN SPEAKING ABOUT A COLLEAGUE. *A*VOID SAYING, "*H*E'S IN THE RESTROOM."

❖ Don't feel you must speak immediately to every person trying to reach you.
❖ Never hesitate to tell a caller, up front, that you only have five minutes.
❖ Avoid becoming too personal or familiar with first-time callers.
❖ Organize your time by having specific hours to take and return phone calls.

ORGANIZE YOUR TIME BY HAVING SPECIFIC HOURS TO TAKE AND RETURN PHONE CALLS.

TRANSFERRING CALLS

Some phone calls are best handled by another person and the caller should be transferred. You can streamline the process by following these rules:

❖ Begin by offering your assistance.
❖ Give the reason you cannot answer the question. Ask permission to transfer the caller to someone who can help.
❖ Only transfer the call if you feel certain the particular person will be of assistance.
❖ Reassure the individual: "I believe Mrs. Grant will be able to assist you."

❖ Give the caller both the name and number of the person to whom you are transferring them.

❖ Stay on the line until the new party answers—or until you know the call has been switched to voice mail. Then quietly place the receiver down.

Also, never forward an office call to someone's residence without first notifying that person. Without such permission, you are invading his or her privacy.

Placing Callers on Hold

In a busy office, placing a person on hold is often unavoidable. In such situations:

❖ When possible, ask for permission to place the person on hold. If the caller is not pleased, or it is going to be more than five minutes, request a number where you can return the call.

❖ Let the caller know why he or she is being placed on hold.

❖ Don't be brusque and say, "Hold on!"

❖ If you place someone on hold, come back to him or her with a progress report at least every 30 seconds.

❖ The first caller should be given priority.

Never forward an office call to someone's residence without first notifying that person.

EXAMPLE: If you are on the phone, have your secretary say, "Mr. Black is on another call at the moment. May I ask him to call you back or would you like to be placed on hold?"

Remember to say "Thanks for waiting" when you return to the line with the information requested by the caller.

NOTE: If a senior executive is calling, always have a signal system in place to let your boss know.

Also, if music is used on the line, be certain it reflects your company's image. Soft instrumental music is usually best. (Always avoid music with lyrics.)

OFFICE ANSWERING MACHINES

When it is impossible to personally answer your office phone, leave a recorded message. For an effective greeting:

❖ Let the caller know your first and last name and the office they have reached.

❖ Make sure your voice is warm, positive, and enthusiastic.

❖ Invite the caller to leave his or her phone number and promise to call back.

❖ State the hours your office is open (or when someone will be answering the phone).

REMEMBER TO SAY "THANKS FOR WAITING" WHEN YOU RETURN TO THE LINE WITH THE INFORMATION REQUESTED BY THE CALLER.

Remember, how you answer the phone on your machine is just as important as how you would answer in person. You are making a lasting impression.

Check your messages several times each day—even if that means access from a remote location. Keep a pad and paper handy to note phone numbers and any action you must take. Make it a habit to delete answering machine messages immediately. Only save a message that contains details someone else needs to hear.

How can I make the most effective use of my voice mail?

*U*pdate the message on your system daily, and sometimes even more often. Don't hesitate to give details of when you will return. For example, "This is Martha. I'll be at a conference until three o'clock this afternoon and will return your call before I leave the office."

Here are more rules to follow:

❖ Arrange to have a "live person" as an option. Say, "If you need help immediately, please call Howard Jones at extension 578."

❖ If you are away from your desk, program your calls to transfer to your voice mail quickly. Otherwise, a fellow employee may think it is necessary to pick up your phone.

IF YOU ARE AWAY FROM YOUR DESK, PROGRAM YOUR CALLS TO TRANSFER TO YOUR VOICE MAIL QUICKLY.

❖ Never allow your voice mailbox to overflow. It doesn't make you look busy, just unorganized.

❖ Become known as a person who returns calls promptly.

Make it a habit to check your outgoing message frequently. You're not making a good impression if your message says, "I'll be back at 2:30 on Monday the 10th," and it is already Wednesday the 12th.

What's considered good etiquette for leaving messages on someone's business voice mail?

*F*irst, don't sound exasperated or upset because you could not reach the person. There's usually a good reason he or she is away from the phone.

Next, never leave more than three messages for the same individual. After that, you become a nuisance.

Finally, let your personality come through the phone. When you smile, it can be heard in your voice.

What general rules should I follow when leaving a message?

*L*et the person know who is calling and what organization you represent. Keep your message short. Speak clearly and slowly.

NEVER LEAVE MORE THAN THREE MESSAGES FOR THE SAME INDIVIDUAL.

Let people know the best time to call you back. Always repeat your name and number twice and conclude with a courtesy— "Thanks" or "Thank you."

HANDLING RUDE OR ANGRY CALLERS

What should be my response to someone who is extremely upset?

If you work in an organization long enough you will probably receive a call from an individual who is agitated and irate. When this happens:

- ❖ Stay calm and polite, regardless of how upset the caller is.
- ❖ Ask, "Would you repeat that slowly so I can write it down?"
- ❖ Listen carefully and express, "I understand what you are saying."
- ❖ Convey your desire to resolve the issue.
- ❖ If you feel the matter is important, arrange to have a company executive call back shortly. Then follow through to make sure that happens.
- ❖ Never argue.
- ❖ If you or your organization is at fault, don't hesitate to admit it.

STAY CALM AND POLITE, REGARDLESS OF HOW UPSET THE CALLER IS.

❖ If necessary, apologize and quickly correct the problem.

❖ Thank the caller for bringing the matter to your attention.

❖ Conclude on a positive note.

Remember, solving the caller's problem or answering his or her request is the key to effective customer relations in your organization.

PLACING BUSINESS CALLS

The key to placing successful calls to any organization is the word respect.

❖ You respect an executive's schedule by keeping your calls brief.

❖ You respect a person's office or position by making the individual feel valued and admired.

❖ You respect a person's dignity by not engaging in gossip or using offensive language.

What are the rules to follow when calling a business executive?

Watch the clock and observe time zones. Calls to offices should be made between 9 AM and noon, and from 2 PM to 4 PM. The

YOU RESPECT AN EXECUTIVE'S SCHEDULE BY KEEPING YOUR CALLS BRIEF.

exception to the 9 AM time is Monday morning—this is when many companies have staff meetings. On that day, call after 10 AM.

Also, avoid calling near closing time. At the end of the day employees are often tired, busy organizing their paperwork, and not mentally ready for your intrusion.

Here are additional guidelines:

❖ When calling an organization, immediately identify yourself and the company you are representing. For example, "This is Bob King with IBM. May I speak with Mr. Walters?" This helps the secretary know who is calling.

❖ Make friends with the secretary. Learn his or her name and, if possible, compliment him or her since he or she can be of great help. Be sincere in your comments.

❖ If it is impossible to speak with the person immediately, share the nature of your request with the secretary. Ask him or her to schedule a convenient time to speak with the executive.

❖ Unless it is an emergency, do not call the executive at home.

NOTE: If someone (such as an assistant) places a call on your behalf, be available to speak immediately. Never keep the recipient waiting.

IF IT IS IMPOSSIBLE TO SPEAK WITH THE PERSON IMMEDIATELY, SHARE THE NATURE OF YOUR REQUEST WITH THE SECRETARY.

How can I add personality to my business calls?

A woman who runs a day care center in Dallas keeps her agenda next to her phone. If a customer says, "We're taking a vacation to Arizona next month," she jots a note on the calendar. You can rest assured that the next time she calls that individual she will ask, "By the way, how was your trip to Arizona? Did you get to the Grand Canyon?"

People love it when you remember the details of their lives. Don't trust your memory—write it down! Let your next conversation reflect on the past, then move forward.

Your phone calls should include more than data and facts. To add warmth:

- ❖ Frequently use the name of the person. "Mary, that's an excellent idea!"
- ❖ Ask questions that touch on family, sports, or community happenings. "Is Johnny still collecting baseball cards? "How is Tiffany coming along with her gymnastics?"
- ❖ Use polite expressions. "Please" and "Thank you" are still in style.
- ❖ Look for opportunities to pay compliments.
- ❖ Smile as you speak.
- ❖ Use vocal variety—avoid a monotone voice.

Never keep the recipient waiting.

❖ Avoid topics of politics, religion, or finances unless that is the intended purpose of the call.

What privacy issues should concern me?

*N*ever pick up an extension phone and listen in on a conversation. And do not discuss confidential matters in an area where you can be overheard. Instead, move to a conference room.

Business Voice Mail

*I*n the previous chapter we discussed voice mail at the home. Many of those same rules apply at the office—plus more.

Make it your objective to become a master of your company's voice mail system. You'll be surprised at what you can accomplish—such as transferring a message to the voice mail of a fellow employee.

Conference Calls

*S*peakerphones have dramatically increased the scheduling of calls with multiple participants. With good equipment, excellent

*N*EVER PICK UP AN EXTENSION PHONE AND LISTEN IN ON A CONVERSATION.

preparation, and an awareness of conference call etiquette, the session will be productive.

What is the protocol for phone conversations when several people are participating?

*S*uccessful conference calls require planning. Ask the participants to arrive a few minutes early so that you can talk about the call before it begins. Make sure every participant has a chair and a notepad, and that all needed documents and materials are in place. Then start the call two or three minutes ahead of schedule to ensure the connection is working and to get "small talk" out of the way.

Here are additional suggestions to make the session more effective:

MAKE SURE EVERY PARTICIPANT HAS A CHAIR AND A NOTEPAD, AND THAT ALL NEEDED DOCUMENTS AND MATERIALS ARE IN PLACE.

- ❖ Be sure to identify every person who is in the room.
- ❖ Each time you speak, identify yourself.
- ❖ Have a schedule and stick to it.
- ❖ A phone with a headset may be helpful for the moderator.
- ❖ Keep paper shuffling to a minimum.
- ❖ Should only one person need to speak, pressing the mute button will help cancel background noise.

❖ During the call, always turn off the call waiting option on your phone.

Remember to avoid putting your phone on hold during the call. It can cause technical problems. Also, try not to use wireless or cordless phones since they often produce distracting noises.

Should speakerphones be used for one-on-one calls?

$\mathcal{D}$o your best to avoid using the speakerphone for personal calls. It picks up background noise and you sound as if you are in an echo chamber. However, there may be occasions when a speakerphone is helpful—for example, when you need to leave your desk to retrieve some documents.

VIDEO CONFERENCES

$\mathcal{T}$he president of a college in Pennsylvania with a branch campus in Atlanta said, "We were spending thousands of dollars for plane tickets and hotel rooms flying executives back and forth for planning sessions before switching to video conferences." He added, "The meetings via television are extremely productive and the man-hours saved has been enormous."

TELEVISION MEETINGS ARE EXTREMELY PRODUCTIVE AND THE MAN-HOURS SAVED HAS BEEN ENORMOUS.

What preparations are needed to make the video conference more effective?

*B*efore the conference practice with the system and test your visuals. Prepare your graphics with large type since television monitors may be small. Prior to the video event, follow these guidelines:

❖ Send presentation materials to participants as hand-outs.

❖ Create a checklist, an agenda and time schedule.

❖ Rehearse basic camera shots.

❖ Establish your backup should the system fail.

❖ Prepare name cards (with bold letters) for each participant.

Also, pay attention to what you wear. Choose solid-color clothing—no patterns or stripes. Avoid blacks and dark reds. Pastel shirts and blouses are better than white. Women should not wear very red lipstick or heavy eye makeup.

What protocol should I follow during the video conference?

*I*f you are the leader, make certain you start on time and introduce all participants at each site. Don't worry about the delay in transmission (usually only one second). Follow these rules:

*P*AY ATTENTION TO WHAT YOU WEAR.

- ❖ Start on time and introduce all participants.
- ❖ Always speak in the direction of a microphone.
- ❖ Look directly into the camera to make eye contact.
- ❖ Ask plenty of questions and show personal interest in every participant.
- ❖ Move slowly so that the camera does not lose you.
- ❖ There should be only one speaker at a time.
- ❖ Allow time for a wrap-up.

A FINAL WORD: Since you never know when you're on camera, avoid nervous habits such as scratching your head or tapping your fingers. And throw out the gum!

OFFICE COMPUTER ETIQUETTE

*H*enry hadn't been at his desk for two minutes when a colleague asked, "How was the party last night?"

"What party?" Henry answered, rather surprised. "How did you know about it?"

"Well, that was the message you left on your computer before you left yesterday," replied the associate.

What was Henry's mistake? He was working in an environment where more than one employee shared the same computer and he failed to log off properly. Here are rules to follow at the office:

ALWAYS SPEAK IN THE DIRECTION OF A MICROPHONE.

❖ Guard your privacy. Assume that all of your messages may be read by associates.

❖ Respect confidentiality. Should you accidentally see a file that is personal, avoid reading the contents and notify the person that the record exists.

❖ Practice a "strictly business" policy. Make a personal commitment that the office computer will be used for company use only.

LAPTOP MANNERS

Don't leave your laptop unsecured.

Company executive meetings have changed. Instead of a group of managers seated at a table with notepads, now practically all you see are laptops.

When using a laptop in the presence of others:

❖ Turn the volume control to "mute."

❖ Never check your e-mail, pull up an Internet site, play an electronic game, or work on a file unrelated to the purpose of the meeting.

❖ Assume those next to you can read your screen.

For security reasons, don't leave your laptop unsecured. If the room is not locked during a lunch break, take the laptop with you.

HANDHELD DEVICES

Personal electronic organizers such as BlackBerries and iPhones are used by millions. They help keep our schedule on track and connect us with the world. At the office, however, we need to make certain their use is appropriate. For example, if you are the only person in a business meeting with a handheld organizer, refrain from its use. It can become a distraction or, worse, you may be seen as a show-off.

Regardless of how dull the meeting, don't use your personal organizer to check messages or write notes about other issues. Also, avoid "playing" with your organizer or checking out its features.

If you need to exchange data with an associate using your handheld device, wait until the meeting concludes. You show your respect to others by giving your full attention to the topic at hand.

Don't use your personal organizer to check messages or write notes about other issues while in a meeting.

FIVE

*F*AX, COPIER, AND PRINTER PROTOCOL

*A*t the start of the electronic age, headlines read, "Paperless Society in Our Future." Well, it did not happen.

In many respects, the opposite has taken place. Fax machines download millions of documents every day, and the proliferation of copiers and printers is unprecedented.

This chapter is a guide to manners when using this special equipment.

FAX ETIQUETTE

*T*he advent of the fax machine had a dramatic effect on the transfer of documents. Suddenly huge numbers of abstracts, records, and reports were being transferred between offices and homes around the world. Many people thought the arrival of e-mail would replace this technology; however, there are situations when sending a fax is the best choice.

Here is how you can make the most of your fax correspondence.

What are the basic rules to follow when faxing?

*I*f you send faxes frequently, you'll first need to get organized. Set up an area near your fax machine with cover sheets, pens, paper, etc. Follow these rules:

Avoid sending a fax in the middle of the night to someone's home.

- ❖ Don't assume everyone has a fax machine. Inquire politely if you need to send a fax.
- ❖ If the document is of importance, make a quick phone call to confirm its receipt.
- ❖ It is always courteous to call before sending a long document. Avoid sending a lengthy fax during peak hours.
- ❖ Be aware that sending a long fax will tie up someone's machine. Consider sending those via email or regular mail.
- ❖ Double check your dialing digits before sending. One number difference could send your fax to New York instead of New Orleans.
- ❖ Avoid sending a fax in the middle of the night to someone's home. The noise can be disturbing. Wait until daytime.
- ❖ Disable your call waiting if it is tied to the same phone that uses the fax machine. Otherwise there may be a disruption.

❖ Limit the size of a fax to a standard 8 inch x 11 inch page. Try to avoid sending legal-size sheets or they may not be received properly.

Finally, never send unsolicited faxes. You are imposing an expense on the recipients by wasting their paper and toner.

What concerns should I have regarding the content of a fax?

*T*he manager of an employment agency gave this advice: "A carpenter always measures twice and cuts once. The same rule should apply to faxes: read twice and send once." It's important to check punctuation, grammar, and spelling before you send a document.

Some other guidelines:

❖ Never read faxes meant for other people. It is an invasion of privacy—like opening mail or listening to a phone call.
❖ Avoid sending jokes to a public fax machine. Someone is sure to be offended.
❖ Do not send business correspondence from your home. If you do, use a personal cover sheet.
❖ Never send a private message to or from a public office via fax. Assume everyone will read it.

Avoid sending jokes to a public fax machine. Someone is sure to be offended.

What details should a fax cover sheet include?

*N*ever send a fax without a cover sheet. It should be simple and easy to read with very few graphics. Be sure it includes:

❖ The date the fax is being sent.
❖ The name (and organization) of the person sending it.
❖ The name of the recipient.
❖ The fax and phone numbers of both parties (should you need to confirm that the fax has been received).
❖ A brief description of what the fax contains.
❖ The number of pages being sent.
❖ Your letterhead should include additional contact information.

How can I improve the graphics in a fax transmission?

I'm sure you have received faxes with photos that look like the inside of a train tunnel, almost solid black. Keep the graphics simple. Intricate logos and fancy borders slow transmission, increase your phone bills, and look unsightly to the recipient.

Here's how to help remedy graphics problems:

❖ If your fax contains photos, test it on "copy" to see what it will look like when transmitted.
❖ Either eliminate the photos or make copies with a "light" setting until the photos duplicate clearly.

YOUR LETTERHEAD SHOULD INCLUDE ADDITIONAL CONTACT INFORMATION.

❖ Line drawings transmit much better than photos.

❖ Heavy dark areas take far too much time to send—and waste costly toner.

❖ Understand that "whiteout" touch up can look like a blotch to the recipient.

❖ Avoid using colored paper. (If the original is on colored paper, photocopy it first in black and white.)

❖ Use readable type—perhaps enlarging before transmission.

With planning and practice, your faxes will both communicate your message and enhance your image.

COPY MACHINE MANNERS

*Y*ou're in a hurry! In a few minutes you have an important meeting and need to make just one duplicate of a needed document. However, when you reach the copy machine, someone with a stack of books two feet high is using the copier—and is treating it as exclusive territory.

When this happens, don't hesitate to ask, "Do you know how long you'll be using the machine? I just need to make one copy."

Whether using a copier at a library, office supply store, or your place of employment, always treat others as you would like to be treated.

*H*EAVY DARK AREAS TAKE FAR TOO MUCH TIME TO SEND—AND WASTE COSTLY TONER.

What etiquette issues should I be aware of when using the copier?

*I*t's important to always stay near the machine while making copies. You never know when an emergency will arise. If the copier has a paper jam, don't simply walk away and expect the next user to solve the problem. Notify a supervisor immediately. Here are other rules to follow:

NEVER MAKE MORE THAN 25 OR 30 COPIES WHEN SOMEONE IS STANDING IN LINE BEHIND YOU.

- ❖ Be considerate of others. Never make more than 25 or 30 copies when someone is standing in line behind you.
- ❖ Never leave the machine empty. Learn how to refill the paper tray.
- ❖ After making your last copy, clear the machine of all special instructions (paper size, zoom, number of copies, etc.). The next user should have a machine set at standard settings.
- ❖ Always remember to remove your original copy.

A final word: The copy machine area at your workplace is not a conversation place. Save the socializing for lunchtime or for after-hours.

PRINTER PROTOCOL

In most offices, printers are a shared resource, usually connected to many computer users. For that reason, we need to be sensitive to the needs of others.

Don't feel the need to print out every page of a computer file. Take the time to view every document online and print only the necessary material. And since printers usually wear out faster than copy machines, avoid using the printer to make multiple copies.

What printer-related issues should I be concerned with?

Your objective should be to see that the work flows smoothly and that you do not monopolize use of the printer.

PROGRAM LARGE PRINT JOBS TO RUN EITHER AT NIGHT OR ON THE WEEKEND.

❖ Don't tie up the printer for hours. Print just a few copies at a time and allow others to enter the electronic queue.
❖ Program large print jobs to run either at night or on the weekend.
❖ Printing during work hours should be reserved for high priority items.

❖ Never turn off the printer unless you have been specifically asked to do so. It can stop the work flow of the entire office.

❖ Learn how to restock paper in the printer.

❖ Never use office equipment for personal use.

Also, avoid loading special papers (glossy, transparency) in a printer. It may damage or jam the unit. Use the copy machine for such work. Also, if you have both a color printer and a black-and-white, use the equipment for its intended use. Never print a black-and-white document on a full-color printer.

*N**EVER** USE OFFICE EQUIPMENT FOR PERSONAL USE.*

What steps can I take to make sure others have equal use of the printing equipment?

*L*earn as much as possible about the technical aspects of computer printing. Understand that complicated graphics are going to take much longer to print, so avoid busy times for such work.

Practice patience! Don't continue to send duplicate print orders if your job is not ready. There may be a long queue and you'll be wasting paper when the printer finally responds.

If the printer does not accept your file, don't automatically resend. Learn the reason for the rejection.

When using faxes, copiers, and printers, always remember that manners are equally as important as machines.

$\mathcal{D}$IGITAL COURTESIES IN PUBLIC PLACES

$\mathcal{O}$n a Florida dental office, a patient motioned for Dr. Leroy McCloud to wait. For the next fifteen minutes the man, seated in the dental chair, chatted on his cell phone.

Finally, Dr. McCloud asked the man to leave the office. "I don't have tolerance for that," said the dentist. Dave Gussow, discussing the problem in the *St. Petersburg Times*, cited these examples of cell phone abuse:

❖ The Parliament in India installed jamming devices to stop members from taking calls in the middle of debates.

❖ Three people have been jailed in Peoria, Illinois because their cell phones rang in courtrooms.

❖ President George W. Bush had to admonish an aide after a ringing cell phone interrupted a meeting with Israeli Prime Minister Ariel Sharon.

Since electronic devices have permeated society, we need to be aware of how we use them in offices, restaurants, on public transportation, and at social gatherings.

AIRLINE ETIQUETTE

 Frequent flyers are often surprised to learn that the rules regarding use of personal electronic devices vary greatly between airlines. Some carriers allow passengers to work on their laptops from the moment they leave the gate, while others make you wait until the plane has reached an altitude of 10,000 feet.

Not all electronic devices are restricted. Airlines have no problem with hearing aids and pacemakers. Most airlines, however, restrict use of some devices during takeoff and landing, including: electronic razors, portable CD players, notebooks, printers, calculators, handheld computer games, video players, and portable DVDs.

Items which are totally banned in-flight include: remote controlled electronic toys, televisions, cell phones, and AM/FM radio transmitters or receivers.

Don't ignore the rules when flying. In some countries, people have actually received jail sentences for refusing to obey electronic flight regulations.

Why can't I use my cell phone on an airplane?

 Some people wonder, "If I can't use my wireless phone in flight, why do planes provide mobile phones for a fee?" The

DON'T IGNORE THE RULES WHEN FLYING.

answer is that the air phones operate on an assigned air-to-ground frequency that does not interfere with the navigational equipment of the aircraft.

To be on the safe side, turn off all electronic devices until you are specifically told you may use them. The moment the aircraft door is closed, turn off your cell phone.

What are the rules of in-flight courtesy regarding laptops?

*A*lthough it may be necessary at times, a cross-country flight is not an ideal atmosphere to work on your computer. And it's certainly not pleasant when the person in front of you suddenly reclines the back of his seat and pushes your laptop into your stomach.

If you must use your notebook, follow these rules:

❖ Request a window seat. You'll find a little more space and you can angle the screen for maximum privacy.
❖ Turn off the volume. The noises may impress your friends, but not your seatmate.
❖ Never pretend the aircraft is your office. Just because the passenger in the center seat is not using his pull-down tray doesn't mean you can seize it to spread out your work.

THE MOMENT THE AIRCRAFT DOOR IS CLOSED, TURN OFF YOUR CELL PHONE.

❖ Don't pull out your notebook until the pilot announces that it is okay to use electronic devices. It's true that computers can interfere with the positioning and communication devices of aircraft.

Here is a word of advice for all passengers: Avoid the temptation to read the screen of your neighbor's laptop. Respect his or her privacy.

What rules should I follow if I use a portable DVD player on a flight?

*A*LWAYS USE AN AUDIO HEADSET.

Some passengers would rather bring their own portable DVD player than watch the in-flight movie. If this is your preference:

❖ Always use an audio headset. Never force your neighbors to listen to something they are not watching.
❖ Position the screen for "you-only" viewing. As with using notebook computers, try to secure a window seat.
❖ Keep quiet! Laughing out loud and making comments to your seatmate is unacceptable.

RESTAURANTS AND ELECTRONICS

A growing number of restaurants are placing signs at the entrance podium that read: "Cell phones may not be used in the dining room. If you need to make or receive calls, please use our pay phone area."

Similar rules should also apply to the use of notebooks and handheld computer devices. The purpose of visiting a restaurant is to enjoy a meal and to engage in polite conversation. Anything that disturbs fellow diners—even those at your table—should be avoided.

While dining, either turn off your cell phone or set it on "vibration" mode. If you are expecting an important call, excuse yourself and keep the conversation short. You show respect to your guests when you give them your undivided attention.

There are additional rules for cell phone etiquette in Chapter One.

Public Phone Courtesies

If you are expecting an important call, excuse yourself and keep the conversation short.

Waiting in line for someone to finish a conversation on a pay phone or courtesy phone (such as in a hotel lobby) can be exasperating—especially if you need to make an urgent call. When you are calling from a public phone, follow these rules:

- ❖ Keep your conversations short; no more than two minutes.
- ❖ If you are using coins to place a long distance call, make sure you have extra change handy.

❖ Avoid placing multiple calls. This is not your office.

❖ Except for an absolute emergency, never ask someone to call you at the number of the pay phone.

Finally, keep your voice volume low. Those nearby don't need to hear your part of the conversation.

ATM ETIQUETTE

Don't be tempted to throw the receipt into the trash container.

It's more than annoying to approach an automatic teller machine and have someone standing a few inches behind you. It is not rude to politely ask, "Excuse me, may I have some privacy?"

Follow these rules:

❖ Stand close to the machine so that the person behind you cannot see the code you punch in or the video monitor.

❖ If you have a large number of transactions to make, return later when the ATM is not busy.

❖ When you have finished, make certain you take your card and receipt with you. Don't be tempted to throw the receipt into the trash container. File or dispose of it properly at home.

❖ Make certain the video monitor has returned to the "home" screen before you leave.

Also, when standing in line, always create a two-to-three foot buffer zone between you and the person using the machine.

CREDIT CARD COURTESIES

At a major department store, the line at the cashier's desk grew quite long when a man's credit card purchase was electronically disapproved. "That's impossible," said the customer. "I just used the card this morning. Let me speak to the manager." Meanwhile, those standing in line grew very restless.

Here are six rules you should follow when using credit cards:

❖ If the customer behind you is paying in cash, allow that person to go first.

❖ Have your card ready before the bill is presented. Don't fumble through your wallet or purse.

❖ Know your credit limit and account balance at all times so that your purchase will be approved.

❖ If, for any reason, there is a delay in processing, offer to step aside and allow other customers to make their purchases.

❖ Always take your receipt with you and compare it with your billing statement—whether from a restaurant or a retail store.

Know your credit limit and account balance at all times.

❖ Never throw a receipt that includes your credit card number into a public trash container.

MICROPHONE MANNERS

*Y*ou may have a great speaking voice and a polished stage presence, but if you don't know how to use a microphone properly, your ability to communicate during a presentation is greatly diminished.

What are the rules for using clip-on or lavalier microphones?

*D*epending on the venue, you may be asked to use a microphone attached to your clothing. If so, follow these guidelines:

❖ Do not attach a clip-on microphone near a piece of jewelry.

❖ To pick up your voice properly, the microphone should be attached rather high on your lapel, tie, or blouse.

❖ Always test the microphone prior to the event.

*D*O NOT ATTACH A CLIP-ON MICROPHONE NEAR A PIECE OF JEWELRY.

What is considered proper use of wireless and stationary microphones?

A microphone, whether wireless or stationary, should be kept at a distance of approximately eight to ten inches from your mouth.

Avoid the tendency to place the microphone directly in front of your mouth. In most cases, the audio signal will be distorted. The ideal location is a few inches below and forward of your chin. This also makes it possible for your audience to see your complete face. Remember, communication is enhanced when people can also read your lips. That's impossible if they are covered by a microphone.

Many professional speakers prefer a handheld wireless microphone since they can pull it away from their mouth (or bring it closer) for emphasis and volume control.

Stationary microphones should not be handled unnecessarily since this can result in unwanted noise.

MUSIC ETIQUETTE

*D*igital downloading, satellite signals, CDs, and iPods have revolutionized the way we obtain and enjoy music. Never has so much entertainment been available to so many. However, there

MANY PROFESSIONAL SPEAKERS PREFER A HANDHELD WIRELESS MICROPHONE.

are standards of personal courtesy in the use of music which need to be obeyed.

Is it bad manners to put on a stereo headset and listen to a CD or portable media player when others are present?

There is a time for social interaction, and a time for private, personal enjoyment. In the presence of others, it is impolite to isolate yourself by listening to music. The exception is when a group decides they will all put on their headphones for a specified amount of time.

IN THE PRESENCE OF OTHERS, IT IS IMPOLITE TO ISOLATE YOURSELF BY LISTENING TO MUSIC.

If the need to listen to your music is of great importance, politely excuse yourself from the room and find a place to be alone.

What should be the response to an individual who loudly plays music from a car speaker system?

Any person who invades the space of someone else is acting rude and discourteous. In most cases, loud music in public places is an adolescent cry for attention.

Many communities have regulations on excessive noise in public places. It should be our task to teach everyone how to treat others with honor, decency, and respect—and that may include reducing the decibel level of music!

VIDEO AND DIGITAL CAMERA COURTESIES

Far too often the user of a handheld or phone camera becomes the center of attention—even more than the person being honored or the event being taped. Here are three important courtesies to remember:

- ❖ Always ask permission of the host or guests before taping a private event.
- ❖ Keep a low profile and learn to be unobtrusive. This may require placing your camera on a tripod at a distance and using the zoom feature.
- ❖ Don't feel you must capture every moment of the occasion. Anticipate the highlights and limit your photo time.

Whether at home or in public, when you truly respect and honor others, good manners will naturally follow.

ALWAYS ASK PERMISSION OF THE HOST OR GUESTS BEFORE TAPING A PRIVATE EVENT.

SEVEN

PARENTS' GUIDE TO ELECTRONIC ETIQUETTE

In the life of a child, a world filled with digital gadgets, wireless phones, and the Internet is as normal as breathing. For parents, however, this technology-driven culture has required a great amount of personal adjustment.

EMPOWERING PARENTS

It is the responsibility of parents and caregivers to make sure their children have the knowledge and understanding of electronic etiquette.

Teach them that the use of electronic media is a privilege, not a right. Permission is given to use such devices when children agree to act in a responsible, ethical, and considerate manner. While the principles of good manners never change, they must be specifically applied to electronic devices.

Why is it important to set boundaries for your children at an early age?

*T*he principles you establish are building blocks that will help shape their character and attitude concerning electronic devices. These courtesies teach young people how to treat family, friends, and others with respect.

Here are parent-child guidelines regarding use of computers, phones, music, and digital games.

COMPUTER ISSUES

*T*he explosion in communications technology—including e-mail and the Internet—has made it possible for children to gain new knowledge and enjoy varied cultural experiences. Plus, computer knowledge is considered essential in preparation for college and career.

As a parent, what are my responsibilities regarding a child's use of the computer?

*H*ere are seven rules to follow:

1. Have a working knowledge of your home computer before allowing your child to have access to it.

*H*AVE
A WORKING KNOWLEDGE OF YOUR HOME COMPUTER.

2. If you aren't computer literate, it may mean taking a short course offered by a computer retail store or a local college.

3. Keep the lines of communication open. Discuss the potential online dangers and instruct your child concerning the responsible use of the computer and online resources.

4. The computer should never be in a child's bedroom, but rather in a highly visible area of the home with the monitor facing the center of the room where parents can view it. Children should not be isolated from interaction with other family members.

5. Visit your child's school and local library and discuss current safeguards they are using to protect the children.

6. Have a discussion with the parents of your child's friends so there is common agreement regarding computer use.

7. Before allowing your son or daughter access to a computer, learn how to install and set age-appropriate security features.

HAVE A DISCUSSION WITH THE PARENTS OF YOUR CHILD'S FRIENDS SO THERE IS COMMON AGREEMENT REGARDING COMPUTER USE.

How effective are filters and "blocking" software in keeping harmful material from being accessed?

A wide range of parental control technologies are available to block content including violence, profanity, hate speech, pornography, drug culture, sex education, gambling, and more. Some even completely prohibit access to newsgroups and chat sites.

Talk with your Internet service provider concerning blocking software and other available controls. They can direct you to programs that have special features, including limiting computer time, keeping a log of all activity, and those that enable parents to decide which applications are to be allowed.

Popular blocking programs include CYBERsitter, Net Nanny, and CyberPatrol. Simply type the words "Internet filters" into any search engine and you'll find a wealth of knowledge.

A note of caution: Many parents make the assumption that electronic filters will keep all unwanted material out of their home. You can never be 100 percent certain. Remember, there is no software that can substitute for the concern and guidance of parents.

Take a proactive approach to your child's use of the computer. You do this by setting appropriate boundaries and adding proper filters and blocks.

Of course, the best protection is for parents to "be there."

TALK WITH YOUR INTERNET SERVICE PROVIDER CONCERNING BLOCKING SOFTWARE AND OTHER AVAILABLE CONTROLS.

What boundaries and rules of etiquette should be set so that my children will have a positive computer experience?

We cannot over-emphasize that appropriate guidelines are essential to the healthy development of a child. Boundaries send a message to children that they are loved—and that their parents care what happens to them. It also helps to build self-confidence because they know what is expected.

Follow these guidelines:

- ❖ Young children should be taught to always ask their parents, "May I use the computer?"
- ❖ Set specific times your child may, or may not, use the computer.
- ❖ Children should never attempt to bypass home computer security devices.
- ❖ Passwords must not be shared outside of the immediate family.
- ❖ Explain to your child that downloading pirated music or unauthorized software is illegal, dishonest, and can result in large fines.
- ❖ Discuss computer ethics with your child. For example: No "hacking" into other sites or experimenting with computer viruses.

Guidelines for Parents

As a parent, how can I help safeguard my child's Internet experience?

In far too many homes, the computer has become an "electronic babysitter" and children spend hours at the keyboard unsupervised. Don't allow this to happen.

PASSWORDS MUST NOT BE SHARED OUTSIDE OF THE IMMEDIATE FAMILY.

Start with a family discussion of the topic and be specific concerning what you consider off-limits regarding Internet use in your home. Follow these guidelines:

❖ If you are not a personal Internet user, learn how to use it. For example, you can personally view the entire history of every site that has been accessed.
❖ Young children should not be allowed to surf the Internet alone—let it become a family activity.
❖ Set limits on the amount of time your child spends with the computer. (We recommend a maximum of one hour per day.) Parental software is available that includes time limit tools.
❖ Time limits should be placed on communicating with friends

NOTE: If your child has access to a computer (in or outside your home) which does not have Internet filters or security devices, make certain you monitor it carefully.

Unfortunately, young people are often vulnerable to exploitation because of the nature of the Internet. It is imperative for parents to know how to protect their families while at the same time benefitting from this new technology.

Young
CHILDREN
SHOULD NOT
BE ALLOWED
TO SURF THE
INTERNET
ALONE.

What guidelines should parents establish for children who use Instant Messaging or e-mail?

*T*each your child that there is a real person at the other end of the message. Always treat that individual with the utmost respect.

Emphasize the fact that e-mail messages are not private. Explain that they are the equivalent of an electronic post card, and are easily accessible by others via Instant Messaging. We recommend a maximum of fifteen minutes per session. Also, to respect the private times of others, IM should be used only between the hours of 9 AM and 9 PM.

Never allow your child to enter chat rooms of unknown individuals. Limit e-mail conversations to a "buddy list." Personally approve the list your child uses with Instant Messaging. Make sure his or her "screen name" is appropriate, and review the profiles of your own child and his or her "buddies" or "friends." Be sure there is no improper or offensive language.

Know your child's passwords and, for safety reasons, check his or her e-mail and "buddy list" regularly.

Remember, you are not simply setting rules, but teaching your children the importance of respecting themselves and their friends.

Never allow your child to enter chat rooms of unknown individuals.

What should I do if my child has been solicited online?

*Y*ou should report any unusual activity coming into your home—the sending of child pornography, attempts to lure a child, posts concerning bomb making or terrorism, or any physical threat. This is prohibited by federal law.

Immediately contact either your Internet service provider, local law enforcement agency, the FBI, or the National Center for Missing and Exploited Children (1-800-843-5678). In such cases, turn off the computer to preserve evidence. Let a law enforcement officer analyze the data on your computer.

A COVENANT FOR KIDS

*Y*ou should ask your child to make the following agreements with you:

- ❖ "I will always ask permission before using the computer."
- ❖ "I will always tell my parents if I see something online that I don't understand."
- ❖ "I will always ask permission before using my full name or sharing personal information online."
- ❖ "I will never give out a credit card number or a password online."

*Y*OU SHOULD REPORT ANY UNUSUAL ACTIVITY COMING INTO YOUR HOME.

❖ "I will not respond to any message that makes me feel uncomfortable."

❖ "I will never call or accept a phone call from someone who has contacted me online."

❖ "I will always tell my parents if someone online asks to meet with me."

❖ "I will not give out personal information about my friends."

Instruct your child never to give a home address, phone number, what school he or she attends—or any data which would allow someone to be able to locate your child.

On the Phone

*T*eaching phone etiquette should begin at age three and continue through the formative years. We recommend purchasing a "play phone" to teach a young child correct phone manners. If early instruction is neglected, the child will develop bad phone habits that are difficult to break.

Start by having practice sessions with your children to teach them to speak clearly and distinctly when on the phone. Children

IF EARLY INSTRUCTION IS NEGLECTED, THE CHILD WILL DEVELOP BAD PHONE HABITS THAT ARE DIFFICULT TO BREAK.

should be taught to know why they are calling and to stick to the subject.

A child should not answer the phone until he or she is old enough to clearly write a message for you (usually around the age of six). The only exception is if you are in the room and are teaching the child to answer the phone.

Show your child how to properly dial 911. Explain the difference between a real emergency (such as a fire or someone breaking into the home) and a non-emergency.

In Richmond, Virginia, a four-year-old was at home on Friday night with the babysitter. Suddenly, the cat slipped out of the door and ran down the street. The girl and the sitter instantly ran after the cat, but a stray dog chased the girl's pet up a tree. Immediately, the little girl ran inside and dialed 911, shouting, "There is an emergency. Something terrible has happened. Please come quick!"

The police arrived about the same time the cat ran home. Later, the girl's parents had a chance to discuss when—and when not—to dial 911.

Should children have their own telephones?

*A*void placing a phone in your child's room. Children should not have a personal phone in their rooms until they are of an age to accept the responsibility to pay for it. Even if a young person

SHOW YOUR CHILD HOW TO PROPERLY DIAL 911.

has his or her own phone and pays for it with an allowance or personal funds, the child must abide by time limits and other rules of phone use.

Long telephone conversations with friends can destroy family interaction and lower school grades.

Cell phones should only be given to children for reasons of safety—not for social calls. We recommend that if a child has a wireless phone, it should be "on loan" and for the purpose of calling home. Children should not be allowed to give the number to friends.

Specifically, what guidelines should I give my child concerning phone use?

*H*ere are ten practical rules:

1. Never enter into phone conversations with someone you don't know.
2. If you are home alone, for safety reasons do not tell the caller, "My parents are not home." Instead, say, "He (or she) is not available right now. May I take a message?"
3. Show your child how to properly use call waiting. It could be an emergency or an extremely important call.
4. Never place an order on the phone using a credit card without permission.

Never enter into phone conversations with someone you don't know.

DO NOT TAKE A CORDLESS PHONE INTO THE BATHROOM.

5. Never place a call from someone else's phone without the host's permission.

6. Do not answer the phone of another person unless you are asked to do so.

7. If you have been given a cell phone or beeper so that your parents can reach you, be polite, respectful, and responsible by turning down the ring volume (or use vibration mode) in public places. Make sure the battery is fully charged.

8. A cell phone call or beeper message from a parent must be returned within seven minutes.

9. Do not take a cordless phone into the bathroom—for obvious reasons.

10. Return the cordless phone to its proper location after every call.

After more than a quarter century of teaching etiquette to young people, the following three rules are considered the most important regarding telephone manners for children:

1. Do not make or receive calls before 9 AM or after 9 PM (or during mealtimes).

2. Calls should be limited to twelve to fifteen minutes, and should be for a specific purpose. For example, to discuss a school assignment.

3. Calls between children are not "just to talk." Also, teach your child how to place and receive calls, and

how to take and leave messages. These are discussed in Chapter Two.

Adults should set the example for their children that the telephone is not for idle chatter or hours of gossip. While we may not think children are listening, they really are—and they will imitate our example. Young people are forming lasting attitudes and patterns for their own behavior. Make sure your conversations are uplifting and positive.

Being respectful of others is a lifelong and step-by-step process that must start early. Always explain why a rule of etiquette is being established and enforced in your home.

ELECTRONIC GAMES

With the excuse that they are "really great for hand-eye coordination," parents have allowed video gaming systems to become electronic babysitters. Unfortunately, excessive use of such games can lead to antisocial behavior. A child is also at risk of being exposed to dangers through the content of the games themselves.

Know exactly what your child is playing with. Many parents are shocked to discover that extreme violence and sexual content are not limited to R-rated motion pictures. Their children may be exposed to the same images on a two-inch screen.

Many parents are shocked to discover that extreme violence and sexual content are not limited to R-rated motion pictures.

The purchase of a game should be made by the parent, not the child. You should personally examine the content of an electronic game before buying it.

Parents must establish these rules:

- ❖ It is rude to ignore the presence of family and friends while engrossed in a particular game.
- ❖ When guests arrive, children should stop what they are playing and engage in polite conversation.
- ❖ Keep the audio volume of an electronic game at the lowest possible level.
- ❖ The family television set is not to be dominated by a child who uses it for a game center.
- ❖ On long journeys by car, set limits on the amount of time a child may use a portable electronic game. Family interaction must remain primary.
- ❖ During short visits with relatives or friends, there will be no playing of electronic games. Instead, children should be involved in conversation.

Don't allow the tail to wag the dog. Game playing should be limited to short periods of time and be seen as entertainment—not something that dominates the life of a child.

WHEN GUESTS ARRIVE, CHILDREN SHOULD STOP WHAT THEY ARE PLAYING AND ENGAGE IN POLITE CONVERSATION.

MUSIC AND YOUR CHILD

A father complained, "I never get to talk with my thirteen-year-old daughter anymore. From the time I get home from work until bedtime, she has those headsets on—listening to who knows what!"

In many homes—by default—the rules have been set by children rather than parents. Perhaps it is time for the family to have a lengthy conversation on the topic of music in the home. As a parent it is your responsibility to establish clear guidelines for use of portable CDs, iPods, and stereo systems, such as:

- ❖ Set the times your children may listen to music.
- ❖ Meal times should be for family conversation.
- ❖ Loud music played on stereos and boomboxes should not become the atmosphere of the home.

In addition, parents should listen to the lyrics of the music their children bring into the home. Offensive language or harmful messages should not be allowed in any form.

The National League of Junior Cotillions screens all music used in its hundreds of chapters nationwide. We believe that positive music can help reinforce the manners we all need to possess.

PARENTS SHOULD LISTEN TO THE LYRICS OF THE MUSIC THEIR CHILDREN BRING INTO THE HOME.

How can I teach my child about the potential hearing loss that may result from listening to loud music?

*P*rior to the teenage years, in the presence of your family doctor, have a conversation with your child regarding possible permanent damage that can result from excessive noise. It's a serious issue.

Here are the facts. When sustained decibel levels exceed 85 for even thirty minutes, hearing deterioration can occur. Amplified rock music is usually between 110 and 130 decibels. We have seen young people "bouncing" and even singing out loud while listening to their headsets in public places. Obviously, the music was too loud.

Teach your child to take these precautions:

- ❖ At concerts, always wear earplugs. You'll still hear quite well.
- ❖ Never stand near a concert loudspeaker.
- ❖ When listening to your personal stereo (either in a room or with earphones) avoid high volumes.

Understand that constant "pounding" music, if listened to for prolonged periods, can result in significant hearing loss.

Teach your child to be aware of warning signs such as dull hearing or ringing in the ear. Even if the symptoms last for only a short time, they are a signal that hearing damage may have taken

*N*EVER
*STAND NEAR
A CONCERT
LOUDSPEAKER.*

place. And remember, the risk of such damage increases with lengthy exposure and greater volume.

James Strachan, the executive director of the Royal National Institute for Deaf People in Great Britain, says, "The evidence is clear—loud music can damage your hearing, and more young people than ever are putting themselves at risk."

When my child is old enough to drive, what rules regarding music in the car should be established?

*A*s a citizen, your teenager must act responsibly—and that should include a parental decision that prohibits blaring music from any automobile in the family.

The issue involves more than respect for others. Many teens are killed on highways every year because their music drowns out the sound of an emergency vehicle siren or the honking of a horn.

Audio headsets should never be worn while driving, And the music volume of the radio must be low enough so that it won't interfere with a normal conversation.

If your teen disobeys the rules you have established, don't hesitate to take away his or her driving privileges. If not, your child may face more serious consequences. For example, in Lakeland, Florida, playing loud music from a car is a criminal violation with up to a $1,000 fine and one year in jail. First time offenders are

Audio headsets should never be worn while driving.

sentenced to "Music Court." Music brings personal enjoyment, yet it should also reflect consideration for others.

While computers, cell phones, DVDs, and digital devices have drastically changed our world, they did not arrive with built-in manners or courtesies. Those must be applied by the users—you and me.

It is our desire that the rules, guidelines, and principles found in this book will be demonstrated as you treat others with honor, dignity, and respect.

Music brings personal enjoyment, yet it should also reflect consideration for others.

THE PURPOSEFUL LIVING INITIATIVE

Smart phones and social networking have created a society where we are "glued" to our devices. Employees are expected to respond to emails immediately and constantly check their smart-phones for updates. Many people update and monitor social networking accounts multiple times per day. Students disregard important classroom lectures in order to message a friend. Parents spend valuable family time after a long day at the office browsing the Internet instead of investing in their children. We are becoming a society who is obsessed with our smart phones and the "connections" they provide. We consider the current level of smart phone use by the average American to be both excessive and harmful to a balanced life.

The dangers of such distracted living are many, ranging from the physical dangers (driving while using a cell phone) to the emotional abandonment felt by a child whose parent's excessive phone use communicates a lack of interest in his or her life. What does it communicate to a child, friend, colleague, or even someone serving you at a restaurant when you choose to look not into their eyes while they speak to you and at a screen instead? Whether we want to admit it or not, doing so clearly demonstrates that what is on our smart phone is our priority.

What, then, are the implications of such skewed priorities? When did Facebook updates become more important than thanking a cashier? When did a text message become more important than welcoming a friend with a firm handshake and a kind smile? When did taking a photo of a meal and posting it to Instagram become more satisfying than enjoying the fragrance and taste of a delicious meal? We are often so busy using technology to document and share the happenings in our life that we forget to live it. We, as a society, seek satisfaction through online connection and find ourselves often disappointed. Is it possible that the satisfaction we seek cannot be found on a small screen or shiny new tablet? Consider the true satisfaction of embracing a loved one after a long absence, accomplishing a goal at work, crossing the finish line of a race, reading the last

We are often so busy using technology to document and share the happenings in our life that we forget to live it.

word of a thought-provoking novel, or enjoying a delicious meal with good friends. Instead of expending so much of our time and energy documenting and sharing our lives via technology, let's refocus our time on purposefully living and enjoying *truly* satisfying experiences.

We would like to propose a "purposeful living pledge" for those who wish to reduce excessive technology use and build meaningful connections instead. Let's join together and practice a more purposeful and less distracted approach to living.

PLEDGE TO LIVE PURPOSEFULLY IN A DISTRACTED WORLD.

- ❖ *I pledge to live purposefully in a distracted world.*
- ❖ *I will make every effort to look my colleagues, friends, and family members in the eye when speaking to them instead of staring at my phone.*
- ❖ *I will build meaningful, personal relationships and not rely solely on social networking to connect with others.*
- ❖ *I will seek satisfaction in my present reality.*
- ❖ *I pledge to never use handheld devices while driving because it endangers everyone around me when I do so.*
- ❖ *I pledge to consider my future when posting anything online and always represent myself with dignity and respect.*

❖ *I pledge to maintain "acceptable use" hours for technology and spend "hands free" time with my family whenever possible.*

❖ *I pledge to take control of mindless smart phone usage and choose to use my time wisely.*

❖ *I pledge to model appropriate, purposeful living and technology use for my family, friends, and colleagues.*

❖ It is our desire to cultivate a generation of intelligent, time-wise citizens who live with purpose and, as a result, achieve great success in all endeavors.

It is our desire to cultivate . . . citizens who live.

$\mathcal{I}$NDEX

ABOUT THE NATIONAL LEAGUE OF COTILLIONS™

The National League of Cotillions™ is the nation's only organization that trains and licenses directors to establish local cotillion programs. The first chapter was established in North Carolina in 1978 and the national expansion of the program began in 1989.

Today, thousands of students are being taught etiquette, social dance, and character education in hundreds of cotillion programs presented by chapters in over 30 states. The programs include:

PRE-COTILLION—pre-kindergarten through fourth grade.

JUNIOR COTILLION—fifth through eighth grades.

HIGH SCHOOL COTILLION CLUB—ninth through twelfth grades.

THE NATIONAL LEAGUE OF DEBUTANTE COTILLIONS™—a post-high school presentation society for young women.

INTERNATIONAL LEAGUE OF CORPORATE COTILLIONS™—special programs for business, social groups, colleges, and universities.

PRE-ASSEMBLIES AND JUNIOR ASSEMBLIES—corporate sponsored scholarship programs for the economically deprived.

To fulfill its mission of making social and character education available in every community, the organization trains and licenses qualified directors who are given an exclusive territory in which to present the program—either on a full-time or part-time basis.

If you are interested in contacting a local chapter in your area, or obtaining information on becoming a director, visit the official Website: www.nljc.com.

THE NATIONAL LEAGUE OF COTILLIONS
P.O. Box 240384, Charlotte, NC 28224
Phone: 1-800-633-7947   Fax: 1-704-846-3232
E-mail: cotillions@nljc.com
Internet: www.nljc.com